Spiritual

Care

and

Therapy

Integrative

Perspectives

Spiritual Care and Therapy

Integrative Perspectives

Peter L. VanKatwyk

Wilfrid Laurier University Press

We acknowledge the financial support of the Government of Canada through the Book Publishing Industry Development Program for our publishing activities.

National Library of Canada Cataloguing in Publication

VanKatwyk, Peter L., 1938–
    Spiritual care and therapy: integrative perspectives / Peter L. VanKatwyk
Includes bibliographical references and index.
ISBN 0-88920-434-9
    1. Pastoral counseling. 2. Counseling—Religious aspects—Christianity
1. Title.

BV4012.2.V35 2003   253′.5   C2003-904093-3

© 2003 Wilfrid Laurier University Press
Waterloo, Ontario, Canada N2L 3C5
www.wlupress.wlu.ca

Cover design by Leslie Macredie, using a sculpture by Derek Green; text design by P.J. Woodland.

Peter VanKatwyk's appendixes (1, 2, 7, and 8) can be reproduced and used by counselors in a clinical context without express permission from the author or publisher.

To Myra

Contents

List of Tables and Figures

Tables

Figures

List of Appendixes

◇ Acknowledgments

Since most of this book has been previously shared, in print and in the classroom, I have benefited from the responses of many people. I experienced the immense value of feedback when I was deprived of it during my sabbatical leave in 1999–2000. In splendid isolation in my native Holland, I struggled with formulating and articulating ideas on which people thousands of kilometres away needed to reflect. I began to better appreciate the meaning of a learning community where knowledge is both unfinished and an ongoing, shared process.

I am grateful to many of my students who enthusiastically participated in the effort to define and develop concepts and practices of spiritual care. As a graduate student, I was fortunate enough to have Howard Clinebell as my teacher and thesis advisor. His generous openness to what the various therapies could offer to human growth and his insistence on inclusivity have been a lasting legacy and an inspiration to the integrative approach of this book. A true mentor, he created a community where teaching and learning are interchangeable.

For over twenty-five years my life has been intricately connected with the learning community made up from the Kitchener Interfaith Pastoral Counseling Centre and the Waterloo Lutheran Seminary at Wilfrid Laurier University. I mention especially my friend and fellow faculty member Thomas St James O'Connor, who kindly consented to write the last chapter of this book on research in spiritual care and counseling, a topic in which he is eminently qualified. Besides students, I thank colleagues who were dialogical partners in envisioning a comprehensive and integrative approach in spiritual care. With special fondness I think of Delton Glebe, who is always poised for wide-ranging theological conversations both playful and profoundly pastoral. When principal and professor of practical theology, he developed the Pastoral Counselling Department of the Waterloo Lutheran Seminary into a leading institution for pastoral counseling and marriage and family therapy programs in North America. John C. Henderson, former executive director of the Kitchener Interfaith Pastoral Counseling Centre, inveterate student and teacher, supported me for additional time in my sabbatical that made the writing of this book possible, and Evelyn Marcon, long-time colleague at Interfaith and the Seminary, provided helpful feedback on many of the chapters.

Family and friends have known how important it was for me to complete this writing project. They have supported me with stubborn interest and, increasingly, apprehension as the book gained the status of an overdue baby. My wife Myra, a clinical professional in the field of child development and protection, read with much faith and generosity everything I wrote and kept rewriting. Her critical insight and good judgment have shaped all the pieces that came together in this volume. She never doubted the eventual outcome of a published work. To her I dedicate this book. Our children, Paul, Trish, Steven, and Martina, who died unexpectedly as a young woman, have composed a rich and ongoing family legacy that has guided me in drawing the contexts of caring (Part 3).

Some chapters have used material from previously published articles and other chapters have subsequently been adapted for publication:

- Chapter 1 has been adapted to "Pastoral Counselling as a Spiritual Practice: An Exercise in a Theology of Spirituality," *The Journal of Pastoral Care and Counseling*, 56/2: 109-119. Summer 2002. It has also been adapted in the chapter "Reconciliation and Forgiveness: A Practice of Spiritual Care" in *The Challenge of Forgiveness*, Toronto: Novalis, 2001.

- Chapter 2 has been adapted to "Preparing A Place—A Theological Reflection on Pastoral Care," *Consensus*, 25/1: 55-66. Spring 1999.

- Chapter 4 has been revised to "What Is the Problem?—Problem Definitions and Resolutions in Pastoral Counselling," *The Journal of Pastoral Care*, 53/4: 409-416. Winter 1999.

- Chapter 5 has been revised to "What to Communicate: A New Chapter in Pastoral Care and Counseling?" *The Journal of Pastoral Care*, 54/3: 243-252. Fall 2000.

- Chapter 6 utilizes parts of "The Helping Style Inventory: An Update," *The Journal of Pastoral Care*, 47/2: 375-381. Summer 1995.

- Chapter 7 follows in part "Healing through Differentiation: A Pastoral Care and Counseling Perspective," *The Journal of Pastoral Care*, 51/3: 283-292. Fall 1997.

- Chapter 8 appears as "Towards a Balanced Whole: The Well-Functioning Family," *The Journal of Pastoral Care*, 55/3: 239-246. Fall 2001.

- Chapter 9 has been adapted to "Marital Therapy for Family Problems: Pastoral Counseling Perspectives on the Process of Change in Constructivist Couple Therapy," *Pastoral Sciences*, 20/1: 143-157. Summer 2001.

- Chapter 10 incorporates parts of a previous article "A Family Observed: Theological and Family Systems Perspectives on the Grief Experience," *The Journal of Pastoral Care*, 47/2: 141-147. Summer 1993.

- Chapter 11 was originally presented as "Parental Loss and Marital Grief: A Pastoral and Narrative Perspective," *The Journal of Pastoral Care*, 52/4: 369-376. Winter 1998.

- Chapter 12 adapts parts of "The Helping Style Inventory: A Tool in Supervised Pastoral Education." *The Journal of Pastoral Care*, 42/4: 319-327. Winter 1988.

◈ Introduction

THE TERM "SPIRITUAL CARE" is made up of two complex reali-
ties, each of which simultaneously connects us to, and disconnects us from, our
lives in the world. "Care," is the very essence of our humanity yet proves overwhelming in its implications: caring involves feeling not only for one's own life
but for what happens in the lives of others and in the life of the world. Care is
energized by the anxiety of living in a finite and unpredictable world—a world
of decay and disappointments. To care evokes the defiance of not submitting to
such a world. To care seeks to transform this world to a safer and friendlier
place. To care strives to bring order and meaning to life. At the same time we
need to counter caring with non-caring. The words "I don't care" express that
we are disheartened by a world resistant to care, matched by our own inner
restraints to go on caring. At times we need to withdraw and disengage from life.
"Not to care" is as essential to life as "to care." Our caring is tempered in
moments of fatigue or depression, times when we need to recuperate from life.
In our daily life we experience health in the precarious balance between "caring"
and "not caring."

"Spiritual" poses another complexity, both placing and displacing us in the
world. The spiritual locates itself in the realm of the sacred. Our need to separate the secular from the sacred, to differentiate the "worldly" from the "other-
worldly," demonstrates our felt incongruity of placing the sacred in the tangible,
ordinary experience of everyday life. Religion performs the task of constructing
places of the sacred for the faith community, focal points for the spiritual formation of life. In religion the sacred is located in the public places, creeds, and
rituals of worship, and is associated with the traditions and discipline of religious practice. Presently, the two concepts of religion and spirituality are sharply
distinguished from each other. Religion is commonly depicted in terms of
organized or institutionalized expressions of faith in shared experiences of
commitment and devotion, while spirituality is often portrayed "as a highly
individualized search for the sense of connectedness with a transcendent force"
(Pargament, 1997, 38). In much of the Western, post-Christian world the decline
of religion has been matched by a resurgence of spirituality as the profoundly
personal quest for enlightenment and meaning. Religion and spirituality can
both be contrasted and paralleled in the specific ways that each pursues the
quest for the sacred. In this book, both a person's religious resources and
unique spiritual orientation to life are seen as valid and active participants in the
practice of care.

The two ambiguous words, when united in the one designation *spiritual
care*, resolve some of the complexities of each word on its own. The two words

need each other to be actualized. Each word interprets and expands the meaning of the other: the sacred appears in acts of caring in a harsh world, and caring constructs the sacred places where people connect and live the meanings of their lives. The assumption of spiritual care is that, despite all evidence to the contrary, the world is a place for caring. Spiritual care embodies the spirit in ordinary human flesh and weaves the sacred into the rough fabric of everyday life.

The term *spiritual care* narrows its focus and assumes a distinct meaning when applied to the practice of caring in the mental health professions and the health sciences. In a clinical context, the pairing of *spiritual* and *care* gains additional ambiguity and complexity. Professional ethics detects an inherent tension between the two domains of the client's religious and spiritual life and the caregiver's professional practice. Respect for the client's rights, convictions, and values has generally marked religion and spirituality—whether the client's or the counselor's—as private areas to be kept off limit in clinical practice. An additional contaminating factor is the common association of religion with spiritual guidance, charismatic leadership, moral instruction, and proselytizing outreach—ways clearly incompatible with accepted clinical standards of practice. A legitimate concern is that spiritual care will become directive in exercising moral and spiritual guidance at troubled times when clients are vulnerable to undue influence and lack free access to their own spiritual resources and autonomous faculties.

The critical tenet for professional counseling is the clinician's awareness and acknowledgment of the power differential between caregiver and client. The potential abuse of the counselor's power is not limited to spiritual care but is present in all therapy, often in direct proportion to the intimacy of the counseling relationship. With regard to the power continuum of the helping relationship (see chapter 7), this book underlines that helping relationships are intrinsically unequal and asymmetrical. This means that when the power of the helper is disclaimed by the illusion that it is not in use, the client is most at risk. This has special urgency for *spiritual care* as a professional practice that emphasizes the personal dimension where both the client and the counselor share who they are and what they value most as human beings. As in other types of therapy, spiritual care practice mixes the personal and professional in the helping relationship. An emerging consensus in the spiritual care literature stresses a nondirective approach where counselors follow the client's direction in spiritual sharing rather than the counselor's (Becvar, 1996; Doherty, 1999). This also cautions therapists against self-disclosure of their own spiritual beliefs without a shared context and clearly established boundaries. As one psychiatrist notes: "Men and women who want to proclaim their private truths at the vulnerable and ill are not physicians" (Fleischman, as cited by Kathy Weingarten in Walsh, 1999, 256). This book focuses on the therapeutic relationship as the place where the professional and the personal meet in the counseling interaction. The *Helping Style Inventory* as the core metaphor of the book maps the various helping postures and proposes the context as the criterion for an appropriate and differential use of the counselor's self in the practice of care.

This book is largely autobiographical, reflecting my wandering vocational journey as a caregiver. I came to America in 1961 as a young theology student from Europe and began my ministry in a Canadian congregation composed of mostly first-generation Dutch immigrants. My pastoral role often coincided with social work in the practicalities of getting new immigrants settled and adjusted to the new country. I encountered anxieties and conflicts that seemed intimately bound to the immigration experience. I also began to wonder whether these problems started with the displacement in the "new country" or whether the immigration also reflected a prior displacement in the country of origin. Conversations with parishioners indicated the post-war transition, financial uncertainties, and family conflicts, as chief among other frustrations often cited as contributors to the decision to migrate.

After eight years in two immigrant congregations, I came into contact with immigrants of a different kind. I started graduate studies with a chaplaincy residency in a psychiatric hospital, followed by more clinical education in a women's prison and a halfway house for women parolees. In these institutional settings displacement dynamics stood out. I began to view patient and prisoner lives in the context of a person's place, or lack of it, in the world. After completing graduate studies, my main vocational identity shifted to the area of counseling. Further clinical education in marriage and family therapy continued to focus on how a person is located or situated in life—the person not as a separate entity but as intricately embedded in and defined by a relational context. Relational understanding of care is especially urgent for those most vulnerable in life. This group increasingly includes all of us, and urges us to social action and ecological stewardship in our threatened, deprived, and fragile environments.

This contextual approach sits well with my other vocational home in pastoral counseling. The tradition of the care of souls, *cura animarum*, centers on the person *in loco*. In the Jewish-Christian tradition, the word "soul" is used to place the person in a context of ultimate meanings where care is not so much organized by the problems of life as by spiritual concerns. Historically it included a variety of helping acts "directed toward the healing, sustaining, guiding, and reconciling of troubled persons whose troubles arise in the context of ultimate meanings and concerns" (Clebsch & Jaekle, 1975, 1, 4). The care of souls tradition is wholistic in its emphasis on the total person: daily and ultimate concerns, body and soul. Later in the history of religious care, the intimate unity of body and soul slowly separated into a hierarchical configuration in which the body represented the manifold ills and afflictions of this world, and the soul symbolized one's eternal destiny in the world to come. The distinction between body and soul became further entrenched in the modern period through the rise of the medical model that claimed specialization in the physical reality of the body, leaving other dimensions of the human condition to be addressed mainly by non-medical specialties of care. Current awareness that every aspect of human life is present in the practice of care has provided a new appreciation for the religious care of souls tradition. There is a return to the roots of spiritual care where soul embraces the whole person in his or her interactions with the world. The literature of spiritual care and therapy demonstrates a growing awareness that our manifold connections in life are essential to the process of healing. Recent studies (Walsh, 1999, Griffith & Griffith, 2002) show that most clients want to share their spiritual concerns in the counseling interaction and resent being split between body and soul: "Clients and persons who have participated in our research have told us that they want to reflect on their spiritual experiences in therapy and that they feel fragmented by attempting to delegate psychological, relational issues to conversations with their therapist and spiritual issues to conversations with their priest or pastor" (Griffith, 1999, 210). In the broad definition of spirituality followed in this book, it is not possible to clearly demarcate the spiritual from other parts of life. Spirituality is at the core of our humanity and runs through all our life experiences and our history of significant life cycle events. I will speak of spirituality not as an entity in and by itself but as a differentiating perspective that simultaneously connects us to and disconnects us from all of life. Like the presence of soul, our spirituality is everywhere and nowhere (Anderson & Worthen, 1994). Similarly the discomfort and challenge of such a broad definition of spirituality is that "a term that means too much soon means nothing—and risks become everything" (Doherty, 1999, 180).

This volume differentiates between *pastoral* care and *spiritual* care. I believe that there are good reasons at this time to go beyond the adjective pastoral, the traditional term for ministry rooted in the Jewish-Christian heritage of religious care. The obvious one is that we live in a world that is ever more transformed into a pluralistic and global community. Hospitals increasingly reflect this new reality in shifting the description of their chaplaincy services from providing *pastoral care* to *spiritual and religious care*. Another reason for reconsidering the adequacy of the term pastoral is the phenomenal rise of the concept of spirituality in the health sciences, clinical psychology, and therapy. The words *soul* and *spirit* have re-entered the world of psychotherapy, highlighting the spiritual dimension of the therapeutic encounter (Becvar, 1996; Cornett, 1998; Emmons, 1999; Moore, 1992; Griffith & Griffith, 2002; Plante & Sherman, 2001). The topic of spirituality is being included in many a therapy course curriculum, some workshop seminars are marketing spirituality as the new frontier in therapy, and an interdisciplinary array of counseling professionals now incorporate the task of spiritual care into their own specialties of care, challenging pastoral counselors to rethink and broaden their own theology and practice of ministry.

I argue for differentiating *spiritual* from *pastoral* care rather than just substituting the term spiritual for pastoral and assign it double duty. Pastoral care and counseling has largely focused on care that is sensitive and responsive to the Jewish-Christian religious traditions and spiritual resources in those who seek the help of caregivers who represent their faith community. I will use the term *spiritual care* for a pluralistic and inclusive practice that reflects on such intrinsic qualities of the human spirit as the yearnings to give and receive love, to find and fulfil one's vocation and potential in the world, and to be grasped by transcendent beauty and transforming values. This sweeping scope radically broadens and democratizes spiritual care: it constitutes the daily expression of ordinary life rather than primarily a religious specialty of care or a professional function of counseling.

The book is perhaps most autobiographical in voicing my personal inclination, heightened by my immigrant experience, to cherish diversity. The book's main ambition is found in its subtitle: *Integrative Perspectives*. It defines the book's inclusive structure of incorporating and networking a diversity of theoretical orientations and practices of care. Rather than develop a distinct model of spiritual care, I follow an eclectic approach that includes spirituality along the full range of essential psychotherapies in individual, couple and family practice. The clinical wisdom of pastoral care traditions and contributions from the rich and extensive pastoral counseling literature are active participants without occupying a position of undue dominance or special privilege.

This book has had earlier lives. Most of the chapters were assembled in a course package, *Spiritual Care: An Integrative Counselling Manual*, for a practicum course which was part of the certification process in the Canadian Association for Pastoral Practice and Education (CAPPE) and/or the American Association for Marriage and Family Therapy (AAMFT). The inspiration for the manual was to develop an adequate integrative knowledge base for a clinical education program in spiritual care and counseling. The focus was to reflect upon the student's clinical case materials in the light of the manual, the text for our seminar sessions.

In another incarnation, I employed the same course package as a text in a graduate course on the models of psychotherapy and spirituality. Again the emphasis was on the text's subtitle: *Integrative Perspectives*. Since integration is about process, the book does not focus on content, on *what* the various counselling theories specifically teach. It focuses, rather, on *how* a particular counselling model fits into spiritual care. The assumption is that the reader has a basic knowledge of the essential psychotherapies and/or that a good sourcebook of the therapies goes along with the text (additional readings utilized in the course included Gurman & Messer, 1995; Corsini, 1989; and Clinebell, 1995).

The present book shows this interaction between the theoretical and the clinical, the interplay between conceptual diagrams and case examples (as a teaching supervisor, I could not help but add appendixes with reproducible diagrams, maps, and summaries).

Part 1 explores the various meanings of spirituality. Current definitions often emphasize the experience of being connected with all of life as the core of spirituality. Connections in living systems, however, are part of a circular process where moments of connection and disconnection reciprocate. Drawing from Paul Tillich's polarity concepts, chapter 1 explores how connections and disconnections coexist and how connections to life lay the foundations for the disconnections that inspire renewed, at times transformed, reconnections: an ongoing cycle where vitality at one polar end empowers the actualization of the opposite pole. Before spiritual care becomes a specialty of professional care and counseling it is an essential function of ordinary life. The first chapter thus focuses on spiritual care as a discipline practiced in normal, day-to-day living. The chapter develops a model of spirituality through the metaphors of places and stories that connect with the sacred when in harmony with a larger perspective of meaning and purpose. It follows a view of spirituality that is both systemic—how we participate in our world, and constructivist—how we map the places of our life and plot our story. The sacred is described in the general terms of a spiritual and transcendent reality, a reality that the Jewish-Christian and other theistic traditions define as God or the Spirit.

Chapter 2, "Spiritual Care in Clinical Practice," focuses on spiritual care in professional practice. The concepts of human places and stories as developed in chapter one are extended to the counseling process. At a halfway house for parolees I met women between places: out of prison yet not part of society. That is where the metaphor of *preparing a place* became a guiding and enduring image for the practice of care. The chapter draws a continuum based on the self-in-the-world schema developed in the previous chapter—a continuum that maps and sorts the various therapy approaches and helping styles in preparing a place.

Chapter 3, "Cross-Spiritual Care," illustrates that spiritual care is not of one kind. Drawing from William James's *The Varieties of Religious Experience* (1902), the chapter explores the diversity in spiritual experiences and argues that caregivers need multiple perspectives to join with people as they talk about their spiritual lives. The chapter profiles the historical emergence of three distinct spiritualities that have become prominent in the practice of care: grace, growth, and resilience. In analyzing the distinctive features of these different spiritual orientations, the languages of spirituality, religion, and psychology are teamed to construct a multidisciplinary spectrum. With this spectrum as a frame of orientation, spiritual care is envisioned as a variant of cross-cultural therapy.

Part 2 develops a comprehensive, largely theoretical overview of the essentials of professional care represented among the various schools of therapy. This section constitutes the centre of the book in its focus on the essentials of spiritual care in the triad of theory, practice, and the helping relationship in clinical practice. Chapter 4 (what to know) describes the major models of therapy as lenses that determine how to see and respond to the presenting problem in counseling. Chapter 5 (what to say) matches different modes of therapeutic language with these various lenses and approaches in therapy. Chapter 6 (what to be) presents the self-differentiation model, proposing an alternative to a dominant reliance on either compassion or competence as a model of care. Chapter 7 presents the synthesis and application of the preceding chapters in Part 2. The *Helping Style Inventory* profiles a diversity of therapeutic relationships that shape the integration of the counselor's expertise of clinical knowledge and techniques with the counselor as a person. It is the critical point where therapy as a science and craft becomes an art.

Practical applications stand out in Part 3 in its focus on the contexts of spiritual care. Part 2 stretched its orientation maps and classification schemas in order to accommodate a wide variety of models of care. Such inclusivity affirms multiple ways of helping and precludes discriminatory prejudgments on what makes good or bad spiritual care and therapy. Exploring the various helping styles with such generosity, however, may suggest that any therapeutic approach will do. Such an assumption serves to pattern models of care after the helper's personal preference, comfort and abilities, or lack of them, rather than after the specific needs of the client. Person-oriented therapy rightly emphasizes that therapy needs primarily to fit the person seeking the help. This therapy is driven by empathy: the presence of understanding and respect in joining the person's inner world of thoughts and feelings. The contextual approach in Part 3 broadens the scope of empathy, seeking to embrace the totality of the person's world, both inner and outer. Such an ambitious and comprehensive approach is pursued through a social systems and family life cycle perspective. From this perspective, good therapy is typified by a sensitivity that is both empathic and contextual.

Chapter 8, "Toward a Balanced Whole," presents an overview of the family systems context for the practice of care. The chapter integrates major family therapy perspectives in developing a comprehensive overview of core dimensions of family functioning and a family assessment diagram. Healthy family functioning is visualized as a balancing act between polar opposites.

Chapter 9, "Textures and Threads," depicts the family as a relational texture that connects and holds the individual lives of its members. In moving through time, the family will pass through critical transition points that often demand radical change. As the family texture unravels, family members hold on to the threads that bridge the life cycle transitions.

Chapter 10, "Endings and Beginnings," describes those changes that not only stretch and tear the family texture but threaten to sever the threads of transition. This happens in crisis events of catastrophic proportions that go beyond normative, developmental life cycle events. In the absence of a sense of transition, the crisis experience is highlighted in the stark contrast between endings and beginnings. Such cut-off points mark the unpredictable, unexpected events such as untimely deaths, chronic illness, natural disasters, and unemployment.

Chapter 11 presents a case of family system grief, *parental loss and marital grief*, following a narrative format. Extensive case studies illustrate all the chapters in this section. The two case studies in chapters 9 and 10 are grounded in actual counseling cases. The Berg family story (chapter 9) is a composite narrative and largely fictional. Identifying details in Maria's case (chapter 10) have been changed for the sake of confidentiality. The story of Martina (chapter 11) recounts a catastrophic loss in my own family.

As the final section, Part 4 focuses on the study of spiritual care both in the personal, experiential learning approach of clinical education through supervision and in the more formal, academic setting of the research methodology that has evolved in studies of spirituality in the health sciences.

Even though most readers may well benefit from the book's progression, it is not necessary to follow its orderly sequence. Some readers may be best directed by their own internal table of contents, organizing the material according to the dictates of their questions and interests. In the service of greater cohesiveness, however, cross references among the various chapters punctuate the text to guide one's way through the diverse pathways of the often unwieldy and uncharted territory called *spiritual care*.

PART ONE

Spirituality
in the
Practice
of Care

CHAPTER 1

▨ Spiritual Care in Ordinary Life

CARING IS AT THE CORE of everything human. It is the awareness of our shared vulnerability and the attendant anxiety about the tenuous nature of our being in the world. Historically, caring arises in the displacement experience of birth: being pushed from the womb, evicted from our lodgment. As human beings we stand out in the depth and length of utter dependency on caretakers for survival. In the aching awareness of its own helplessness, a small child will tenaciously cling to others through "attachment behaviors" (Bowlby, 1979, 1988). The search for security continues as a lifelong practice of tending to our safety in a world filled with frustrations and uncertainties. Anxious concerns and insecurities lead us to seek out trusted caretakers whenever we feel threatened in our ability to manage and take care. In time we discover the joy and empowerment of caring as a reciprocal process. In mature attachments we experience mutuality in relationships when we simultaneously care and are cared for. In psychosocial developmental theories, we are measured by what we care for and for whom we care. In Erikson's (1964) vision of human growth, the thrust of life is toward the generative stage where we direct ourselves to the central task of caring for the next generation.

Spirituality is often defined as being connected to all of life. The focus on connectedness is the common link between *spirituality* and *care*. Appreciation for the common things in life and concern for each other in our daily relationships create a connected self. Gilligan (1982) defines healthy development in the relational terms of an ethic of care that is guided by sensitivity to others. The assumption is that the everyday world is a place for caring and that spiritual care embodies spirit in ordinary human relationships in life.

Theologies generally trace the beginning of all things to a God who after creating a world calls human beings to take care of it. Psychologies focus on the beginning of life at the moment of human birth, when an alien and noxious world is transformed by the hands of caring. In the context of beginnings, theologians and psychologists can meet each other in the story of *Genesis*. In the words of T.S. Eliot, without a "place of lodgement and germination," our world remains "waste and void":

> In the beginning God created the world. Waste and void.
>> Waste and void. And darkness was upon
>> the face of the deep.

And when there were men, in their various ways,
    they struggled in torment towards God.

Blindly and vainly, for man is a vain thing, and man without
    God is a seed upon the wind: driven this way and that,
    and finding no place of lodgement and germination.

                    —from Choruses from "The Rock" (1934)

A Place

While religion is commonly identified with organized and communal places of the sacred, spirituality is marked by the deeply personal experience of finding one's place in the world, a place of lodgement and germination. Such a place establishes personal identity in the pursuit of one's true
objectives and possibilities in the world. The existentialist theologian Paul
Tillich (1963) describes the process of creating a place in the world through the
polarity of individualization and participation. It depicts the circle dance of the
self and the world in connecting to and disconnecting from each other. It is the
process by which all living things establish their place in their world. In the
process of self-integration, "the center of self-identity is established, drawn
into self-alteration and re-established with the contents of that into which it has
been altered" (30).

Figure 1.1   One's Place in the World

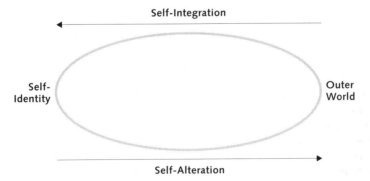

This graphic description depicts the cyclical movement of the self reaching
out, participating in its world, connecting with its possibilities and being
changed in that encounter, then returning to its center of identity. One's place
in the world is not static but rather a dance of constantly balancing one's participation in the world with one's personal center of identity. Tillich calls this
the process of self-integration as it moves between the personal center and the

manifoldness of its surrounding world that is taken into the self. This move-ment of self-integration is life in contrast to disintegration that leads to death.

Tillich's systemic philosophy of health and disease fits the biological dimension of life in terms of the organism's participation in its environment balanced by its resting in its own center. The same dynamics equally apply to the realm of the human psyche and spirit. Murray Bowen's natural systems theory is similar to Tillich's philosophical description of self-integration as a dynamic equilibrium between polar opposites. Bowen (Kerr & Bowen, 1988) posits two biologically rooted opposing life forces: one that propels an organism to follow its own directives and be a disconnected entity, the other that propels an organism to follow the directives of others, and be a connected entity. For the human self that means that there is one instinctual life force toward *individuality* and another life force toward *togetherness*. The goal of human development and spiritual maturity is to become a balanced or *self-differentiated* human being, to be an I while connected to others.

The process of becoming a self, as described in the dialectics of self-integration or self-differentiation, is part of a larger spiritual endeavor, a process of establishing one's sacred place in life. Being in place is a process of balancing care for self with care for the larger world in which the self participates. This applies not only to the individual self but also to intimate social systems such as marital and family relationships. A relationship has its own inner identity and calling in life that is expressed in a similar process of establishing its place in the world. A parallel process takes place between the relationship as a whole and the separate selves that constitute the relationship. Balanced interplay between the life forces of individuality and togetherness is crucial if the household or couple is to experience an emotionally and spiritually significant relationship. If a relationship is a place of lodgement and germination it becomes a sacred place where both the self and the relationship can flourish.

Like the concept of the soul, the meaning of a sacred place resists the confinement and clarity of rational definition. Intuition and imagination might be better sources for knowing the sacred. However, the concepts of self-integration and self-differentiation sketch a profile of basic characteristics of a sacred place. Self-differentiation emphasizes the need for a sacred place to be bounded in a centered and well-defined self. Thomas Moore (1994) diagnoses the lack of personal boundaries as a primary soul-disorder called "psychological modernism." He defines this spiritual malaise as: "An uncritical acceptance of the values of the modern world. It includes blind faith in technology, inordinate attachment to material gadgets and conveniences, uncritical acceptance of the march of scientific progress, devotion to the electronic media, and a lifestyle dictated by advertising" (206).

Self-integration is also about boundaries but emphasizes the flow back and forth in a continuous process of growth and change. Rather than closed and rigid, the boundaries are permeable like the membrane of a living cell. From this perspective, the experiences and memories of everyday life shape and energize our sacred places. To return to Moore (1994): "Spirituality is seeded, germinates, sprouts and blossoms in the mundane. It is to be found and nurtured in the smallest of daily activities...the spirituality that feeds the soul and ultimately heals our psychological wounds may be found in these sacred objects that dress themselves in the accoutrements of the ordinary" (219).

A Story

Sacred places are not stationary and isolated. They are connected and configured into compositions. Sacred places map a landscape and plot a story. Israel is called the Holy Land because its geography is dominated by sacred places, places that are documented and organized into narratives. Sacred places are marked, claiming that particular life space as spiritual territory. The Hebrew Scriptures tell the story of the fugitive Jacob, sleeping on foreign soil with a stone as his pillow. That night he dreamed of a ladder connecting earth and heaven, with the angels of God ascending and descending on it. When Jacob awakens the next morning he says: "Surely the Lord is in this place—and I did not know it!" (Genesis 28:16, NRSV). Jacob marks this place as sacred with a pillar, his stone pillow, and calls the place Bethel, the house of God. Jacob's life is told through the narrative thread that connects the sacred places in his life, from Bethel to Peniel, the face of God (Genesis 32:30), where Jacob wrestled with God and his name was changed to Israel. Sacred places are the marker events in the story of our lives. When the story is life creating and name changing, we know that the place where it happened is sacred.

The self-integration schema emphasizes an ongoing and reciprocal cycle in which the self lets go of itself in self-alteration only to re-establish itself as a centered self. This is the function of "self-creation," that is "growth within the circular movement of a self-centered being and growth in the creation of new centers beyond this circle" (Tillich, 1963, 31). The self never returns to the same center after having connected with the outside world and the world is never the same as the self returns to it. Such a conceptualization views the self as a movie or a narrative: a series of self-world interactions over time in a variety of settings with an organizing theme. Such a process is articulated in a story or script that maps and highlights the marker events of a life. Our story is not a recitation of events that happened to us in the past. Life stories are intensely present, active, and creative realities. In our stories we selectively and subjectively organize our life experiences, sorting them into chapters and titles, introductions, and conclusions. Stories are meaning-making constructs by which we write up and view ourselves and our world under particular headings and themes.

This is the central argument in the psychology of human development. In life cycle theory, persons and relationships develop through the process of negotiating new worlds, encounters that chart the geography of significant places and story the journey of our lives. In Erik Erikson's psychosocial life cycle perspective, human development can be read as the process of soul-making (1994, 109-159). His schema depicts a developmental process through which the person gains the "virtues" or "strengths" appropriate for ever-widening social interactions. Hope, will, purpose, and competence become the rudiments of virtue in childhood, fidelity the adolescent virtue; and love, care, and wisdom the central virtues of adulthood.

We are shaped by the marker events of our lives, some developmental, others unexpected, sometimes catastrophic, events. To honor the sacred in a person's life is to attend to these family and personal stories. These are the sacred scriptures found in diaries, saved letters, special objects, and photo albums recording the significant times and places in one's personal and family history. This is what gives many autobiographies their special fascination as selective histories of life shaping and life changing events.

A Harmony

The focus to this point has been on the places and stories that ground the sacred in everyday life. This here-and-now, time-and-space focus stresses that the sacred is immanent in everyday life. The sacred, however, is present with transcendent power. Seeking harmony with this transcendent sphere has been a perennial inspiration for religious sentiment. The English composer Henry Purcell in his *Ode to St Cecilia* (1692) attests to music's cosmic significance:

> Thou tun'st this world below, the spheres above,
> Who in the heavenly round to their own music move.

William James quotes the stoic philosopher and Roman Emperor Marcus Aurelius: "Everything harmonizes with me which is harmonious to thee, O Universe. Nothing for me is too early nor too late, which is in due time for thee. Everything is fruit to me which thy seasons bring, O Nature" (1960, 51). This prayer carries an ecological sensitivity and relational ethics that binds us to all of life. According to William James this sentiment is expressed with even more passion in theistic religion where the invisible world of the universe is the realm of a personal God who desires harmony and actively seeks such intimate connection with humanity. Psychologist Allen Bergin, prolific author of research studies in religion and mental health, follows a harmony approach in his major premise that:

> God exists, that human beings are the creation of God, and that there are
> unseen spiritual processes by which the link between God and humanity may
> be maintained...We define spirituality as attunement with God, the Spirit of

Truth, or the Divine Intelligence that governs or harmonizes the universe...We assume that human nature includes spiritual capacities, i.e. ways of responding to, harmonizing with, or acting on the promptings, enlightenment, or sense of integration that may be associated with the Spirit of Truth" (1998).

The *harmony* concept, however, is not confined to theistic constructs. Erikson's life cycle theory is an example of spiritual humanism, positing the existence of a basic intelligibility and life pattern in the structure of the universe to which human growth processes conform. Erikson's schema of human development is based on the "epigenetic principle" that "anything that grows has a ground plan, and that out of this ground plan the parts arise, each part having its time of special ascendancy, until all parts have arisen to form a functioning whole" (1968, 92). This ground plan is comprehensive, guiding human life as it evolves toward biological, social, psychological, and spiritual maturity.

In Tillich's schema, the circular movement of *self-integration* produces new centers for the self that map the horizontal line of growth in human *self-creation*. Tillich adds the new dimension of *self-transcendence* that strives "in the vertical direction toward ultimate and infinite being" (1963, 86). In this visual representation, "the vertical transcends both the circular line of centeredness and the horizontal line of growth" (1963, 86). In Tillich's systematic theology, these three functions of life relate to the three basic polarities of being: self-integration on the polarity of individualization and participation, self-creation on the polarity of dynamics and form, self-transcendence on the polarity of freedom and destiny. These three life functions correlate with the three dimensions of the sacred explored in this chapter and depicted in Figure 1.2: the *sacred place* of establishing a personal centre and vocation in the world, the *sacred story* of connecting sacred places through a cohesive theme, and *sacred harmony* of reflecting the depth dimension of life experience.

It is evident in human experience that though these three dimensions of the sacred can be conceptually distinguished from each other, in life they cannot be separated but meet in balanced unity. The sacred is embedded in everyday life through the mediating power of the human spirit. An encounter with the sacred is felt in a commitment to a life of "inclusive caring" (Mayeroff, 1971). A "spirit person" (Borg, 1995) is the unique individual to whom the sacred is an immediate and totally encompassing, experiential reality. Most of us have no such direct access to the sacred, yet the human spirit, individually and communally, grasped by the transcendent power of being, can experience the sacred in the ordinary. Mediation of the sacred is found in living religious traditions celebrated in worship and appropriated in such religious practices, as prayer and meditation. Beyond religious practice, the human spirit is playful and infinitely resourceful, able to engage countless mediators of the sacred in encounters as disparate as a sunset, a piece of music, the loss of a loved one, a warm bath, children at play, and the silence of the night.

Figure 1.2   Dimensions of The Sacred

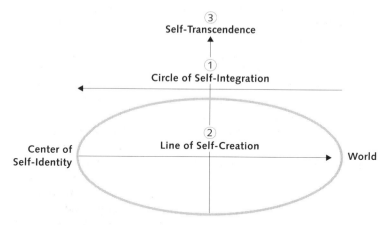

1. **Self-Integration:** the *sacred place* of establishing a personal center
2. **Self-Creation:** the *sacred story* of connecting a line of sacred places
3. **Self-Transcendence:** the *sacred harmony* of reflecting the vertical beyond

Clinical Reflections

This chapter has focused on spiritual care in everyday life through establishing and tending one's place in the world. What is implicit in spiritual care in ordinary life, however, becomes explicit and intentional in the professional practice of care. Clinical practice also seeks to establish a place of lodgement and germination. The British psychoanalyst Donald Winnicott (1965) developed the concept of a holding environment—the care of the parent that envelopes the dependent infant in preparation for the rough ride through life's unexpected bumps and solitary transitions. Winnicott and others have applied this same term to the counseling relationship as a place of safety that, paradoxically, prepares for going it alone. The term holding environment carries spiritual meaning: care as both a sanctuary from destructive forces and a launching pad for new life.

Allen Bergin (Richards & Bergin, 1997), a one-time research associate of Carl Rogers, has coined the term *meta-empathy* as the presence of a transcendent spiritual guidance and enlightenment for the counselor. He defines meta-empathy as "an openness to inspirational impressions that convey spiritual insights or convictions about the individual that differ from ordinary diagnostic categories or treatment hunches" (1998, unpublished lecture, see references). In meta-empathy both the client and the counselor find a safe place, a therapy-friendly universe that fosters a sacred alliance between therapist and

Spirit in co-therapy. Prayer and silent reflection are often relied on as the traditional tools in the process of attunement to a spiritual presence.

Toward the end of his life, Carl Rogers (Thorne, 1992) wrote about a mystical, spiritual, fourth dimension in which the three core conditions of caring—congruence, acceptance, and empathy—culminate. In spite of a life-long caution and suspicion of religious language, Rogers refers to the discovery of "transcendent" moments in the process of the counseling interaction: "At those moments it seems that my inner spirit has reached out and touched the inner spirit of the other. Our relationship transcends itself and becomes a part of something larger. Profound growth and healing and energy are present" (Rogers, 1986, 198). Rather than isolate the spiritual dimension as a separate category, we can say that all expressions of caring presence harmonize with the mystery of invisible healing energies of a transcendent order. From this perspective, the practice of spiritual care is about a spirituality not floating in abstract ideals, split from the body and our daily lives, but grounded in the concreteness of earthly places and in the reality of relationships in the everyday world.

Conclusion

In this chapter's effort toward a philosophy of spirituality in ordinary life, I have become aware how autobiographical one's view of spirituality is. In the above exposition I see my own story as an immigrant (the need to establish one's place in the world and connect with one's best possibilities in the new world), my discipline in family therapy (a relational and systemic definition of spirituality) and a taste for the polarity theology of Paul Tillich acquired in my graduate studies in religion and psychology. In terms of Paul Jones's (1989) mapping of Theological Worlds, my image of spirituality largely resides in the world of separation and reunion. Its markers are found in wholeness and harmony, in the integration and transcendence of the polarities of life, and in the circle dance of dis-connecting and re-connecting with one's world.

This chapter's conceptual exercise demonstrates that each person's spirituality is particular and limited. Unlike pastoral care, which reflects religious traditions of care and accountability to a faith community, spiritual care is broader in scope in its interdisciplinary reflections on human existence. Spiritual care embraces multiple spiritualities and bridges diverse theological worlds. This chapter provides a sample or case study of one personal statement or philosophy of spirituality, seeking to encourage other practitioners to discern and articulate their own model of spiritual care. Such an exercise primes the awareness process of making explicit what implicitly informs one's practice of care. It may also bring out points of discrepancy between what we believe and what we practice, measuring the level of congruence between one's espoused theory of spiritual care with the actual practice of care in use. This challenge in self-awareness is further pursued in chapter 7, which profiles the *Helping Style Inventory* as a conceptual tool in self-monitoring and as a catalyst in the critical reflection on the beliefs and practices of spiritual care.

CHAPTER 2

Spiritual Care in Clinical Practice

THE PREVIOUS CHAPTER looked at spiritual care as a basic quality of ordinary life, as a universal practice of establishing and tending one's place in the world. In this chapter, spiritual care will have a more narrow and specific focus as an expression of clinical practice in caring for others.

The word "clinical" derives from a Greek word meaning "at the bedside." For centuries professional formation in medicine involved learning not only through books and lectures but also through a supervised practicum, face to face with people in need of care. More recently, this model of clinical education spread to such other professions as social work, law, and psychology. Theological education moved to the clinic of the hospital in the development of clinical pastoral education in the 1920s, to study the human condition not through written texts but through "living human documents" (see chapter 12).

A clinical context for caring, however, does not change the basic meaning of caring as the mark of being human. Caring is not what distinguishes the spiritual caregiver or professional helper from other human beings. In fact, what we designate as unique about the helping professions—caring—is precisely what is most common and fundamental about being human. Caring is about how a person evolves as a human being. It is rooted in our birth and introduction to our first caregivers, followed by an ongoing history of relationships weaving the psychological and spiritual textures of care from which we are born again and again into the human family. In a time of increasing awareness of the fragility of our planet in conjunction with the disparities and diversities among its people, caring is a systemic concept including both the intimate sphere of interpersonal relations and the larger social, environmental, and political contexts of our lives. In timeless words written a generation ago, Milton Mayerhof defined the meaning of caring through the topographical metaphor of being "in place" in the world:

> In the context of a man's [sic] life, caring has a way of ordering his other values and activities around it. When this ordering is comprehensive, because of the inclusiveness of his carings, there is a basic stability in his life; he is "in place" in the world, instead of being out of place or merely drifting or endlessly seeking his place. Through caring for certain others, by serving them through caring, a man lives the meaning of his own life. In the sense in which a man can ever

be said to be at home in the world, he is at home not through dominating, or explaining, or appreciating, but through caring and being cared for. (1971, 2)

The above image of being "in place" in the world will be the guiding metaphor in this chapter on spiritual care in the professional practice of "preparing a place."

A Place to Be

Being human and having a place are not distinct and separate realities. How we are located in the world, in the multiplicity of our relationships, defines us as human beings. Places determine not just where but who we are.

The Genesis myth tells how the Creator fashioned the human being from the dust of the earth and called the human species by the collective noun *adam*, "of the soil." The story tells how God planted a garden and settled Adam in this place. Adam's vocation is to tend the garden and live in community, split at the side to become a couple and multiply.

This is the story in the beginning chapters of the Hebrew Scriptures: an idyllic picture of people not ashamed in being naked, at home with each other and in place in the garden. Then follows a collection of stories of human displacement and migrant journeys. Displacement is the theme of the story of the fall. God calls Adam: "Where are you?" As Paul Tournier comments in an engaging book on the significance of human places: "Adam hid himself. The place had already ceased to be paradise for him. His hiding-place among the trees was not his place, but an alibi ... He had already begun to flee from place to place" (1968, 39).

After the fall, the God of creation becomes the God of care, preparing a place for those who have none. God is the God of Abraham, Isaac, Jacob, and Joseph—Genesis migrant stories leading to the Exodus story of the migration of a whole people. The Exodus story has become a cultural epic in the Western world. The Hebrews are displaced as slaves in a foreign land, their future cut off by pharaoh's command to kill their male children at birth. God hears the people's cry of desperation and sends Moses, a survivor of pharaoh's ethnic cleansing, to guide them to the land promised to Abraham.

The Gospels reflect the same migration theme in telling the Jesus story. It follows the story of Joseph who was sold as a slave by his brothers, but who ends up as ruler of Egypt and feeds his people in a time of famine. The Moses story of the wilderness wanderings of the people of Israel gets a retake in the account of Jesus temptations in the desert. The desert represents the non-place of deprivation, staging devilish temptations of bread, the kingdoms of the world, and power. The story of Jesus's resurrection and ascension becomes a migration story that takes on cosmic proportions. In the Gospel of John, Jesus is the one who prepares a place with God: "In my Father's house there are many dwelling places. If it were not so, would I have told you that I go to prepare a place for you?" (John 14:2) From this perspective, earthly places become provisional and penultimate.

A case example: The Tom story

Tom, a 34-year-old man, is admitted to the hospital after an apparent suicide attempt with religious delusions. Tom's wife reports that she comes from a prior marriage and is still impacted by her first husband's rejection and his ongoing interference in the present marriage through disputes about support payments. In order to gain some space for their relationship, the new couple had moved to another state where Tom who, with a master's degree in library science and a Ph.D. short a dissertation, secured a job as a librarian. After some work-related conflicts, Tom accepted a university library position several hundred miles away, a position that soon was terminated in a reorganization of the institution. He was unsuccessful in locating employment for over a year, even though he applied for a variety of positions throughout the United States.

A few weeks before his hospitalization, Tom had returned to Atlanta to visit his parents. At this point he had received "a divine message" convincing him that a position at a public library in Atlanta would be offered to him. Tom grew up in Atlanta alongside a younger brother who was popular with friends and the shining star of his parents, in sharp contrast to Tom's withdrawn and socially inept demeanor. However, Tom did well academically and went well beyond his brother in advanced graduate work.

When Tom failed to land the Atlanta librarian position he developed further religious illusions, increasingly identifying himself with Jesus. In a visit to the parental home, Tom, in a sudden state of agitation, jumped out of a second storey window, fortunately to land in some dense bushes.

The dynamics of displacement tell the Tom story. Having regressed to the perceived inadequate child position in the parental home, he literally displaces himself by jumping out a high window. His childhood experience continues to dominate his adult work and love relationships. In his marriage he is displaced by the first husband in the same way that he as a child felt overshadowed by his younger brother. The first husband never leaves the marriage but occupies the mind of his ex-wife, interfering in the new marriage by ongoing disputes. Tom's major life strategy, academic compensation for a life of social maladjustment, fails to secure a place in the workplace. His chosen world of books does not build a secure base. The cruel stripping process culminates in a year of dislocating moves across the country and failed job applications.

The place of religion forms an intriguing part of Tom's story. The father of the clinical pastoral education movement, Anton Boisen, reframed the disorientation in emotional disturbance as a human struggle to solve spiritual and ethical problems. He believed that psychological disorders could manifest the process of seeking reconciliation and restoration; that madness can be the soul's journey to wholeness. In his autobiography (Boisen, 1960) he describes in painful detail his own psychotic delusions and makes sense of them as a religious search for personal integration.

Tom's identification with Jesus is open to a variety of interpretations. The language of psychology describes Tom's experience in terms of the crisis impact of environmental stressors on his fragile self-definition, with dissociation as a defense mechanism. In his religious delusions Tom adopts Jesus as an icon of grandiosity. In the hospital, however, Tom could begin to re-evaluate his faith in a search for a religious reorientation in the world. Stepping out a second story window can be perceived both as a step of suicidal despair and as a grandiose step of faith in transcending earthly non-places.

A Place to Prepare

In the previous chapter, spiritual care was described in its connection with the sacred. As stated, the counseling relationship has the potential to offer such a sacred connection, with moments when the relationship appears to transcend itself and become larger than itself. Counseling theories often identify the healing dynamic in the caring relationship itself: it is the relationship that heals. In the counseling interaction people "prepare a place" for each other. It is a joint project: the client opens his or her life story for the counselor, and the counselor clears a therapeutic space for the client through his or her attentive presence.

It is ironic that human relationships constitute the main source for both trauma and healing. Sometimes people have been hurt so deeply in their relationships that they have built impenetrable barricades around themselves. Most of us are cautious in maintaining a "safe distance"—from some people more than others. Yet, in times of suffering or confusion, we are drawn to seek out a "place" in the confidence of other people. Conversely, in the process of preparing a place for others, we find our own place in the world. Preparing a place for another human being is patterned after our mother's womb—the place of preparation. In love and caring relationships we experience a similar birthing process.

In 1959 Carl Rogers presented his conclusions about what makes a therapeutic relationship a safe place where growth will take place. He maintained that the relational triad of congruence, acceptance, and empathy will create a therapeutic space or climate in which healing will naturally follow. It is remarkable that arguably the most influential psychologist and therapist of the twentieth century represents in these three core conditions of therapy the old traditions of spiritual care. Each of these three core conditions (see Appendix 1) center on the theme of preparing a place:

- In *congruence* the caregiver is present as a real person, rather than the pseudo-presence of one hiding in the role of the professional or expert. The helping relationship is not a clinical one of scientific detachment but a real one of genuine, personal presence. The counselor is co-present, both to the client and to himself or herself, and thus can draw from the fullness of the counseling relationship.

- In *acceptance* the counselor prepares a place of positive regard of and belief in the other. The core task of religion may well be located in the symbols and rituals representing the sacred place of acceptance. To meet in mutual confirmation is a universal human need, and the essence of love. In the context of a person-centered counseling relationship, there is the analogy of the transcendent place offering full attention and unconditional acceptance. The caregiver provides a presence that symbolizes an enduring place.

- In *empathy* the counselor is attuned to the client's inner world of feelings, thoughts and yearnings. This entering the other's perceptual world seeks to understand what it is like to be in that place. This empathic entry enlarges and transforms the client's world into a place where that person can be at home. Rogers defined empathy as a potent therapeutic force and compared it to a birthing process of securing a place of belonging: "It releases, it confirms, it brings even the most frightened client into the human race. If a person can be understood, he or she belongs" (1986, 129).

There is almost a mystical, if not romantic, intensity about these core conditions. A valid criticism is that such a counseling relationship is so superior to most other relationships that therapy can become an end in itself, a substitute for real life. Intimate moments generated by the core conditions can easily degenerate to an idealization of the affirming and loving stance of the counselor. This in turn can open the way to dependency distractions or romantic distortions that can then easily lead to abuse of these client vulnerabilities. It is important to note that Rogers emphasized that these are *facilitative* conditions intended to promote the self-realization of the client. It is the paradox of Winnicot's concept of *holding environment*, where the client is not held back but empowered and released to "go it alone." The Rogerian process of facilitation often focuses on the non-directive stance of the counselor that frees the client to spontaneously find his or her own way. I believe that a more helpful facilitation occurs when counselor and client interact and collaborate in the therapy. To prepare a place is a joint enterprise of active co-operation within the bounds of respect for client autonomy.

To Bind and to Release

Tillich's description of the self is one of perpetual motion and change. As described in chapter 1, the self from the center of personal identity draws into self-alteration when connecting with the surrounding world, then re-establishes itself in a new center that incorporates the changes of the self-alteration. In this conceptualization, the self's place in the world is not static but an expanding process of self-creation balanced between the two poles of self-alteration and self-identity.

Following this diagram (Figure 2.1), the self's place in the world can be plotted on a continuum between two polar ends, each becoming terminal when not balanced by the other. In Tillich's description, the one terminal end is the death of mere self-identity, the other, the death of mere self-alteration. Mere self-identity is to be bound in an immovable center without a growth process of adaptation to the surrounding world. The opposite is mere self-alteration with no return to the centre in self-integration, resulting in a lost center due to the dispersing impact of the manifoldness in the surrounding world. In the following figure of the self-in-the-world continuum, I represent the death of mere self-identity as the *contained* self and the death of mere self-alteration as the *dispersed* self.

Figure 2.1   The "Self-in-the-World" Continuum

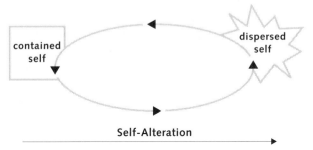

This differentiation between the "two ways of death" has been graphically described in the history of family systems. Beavers and Hampson describe two opposing styles of family functioning in the following definition: "Centripetal (CP) family members, looking for satisfaction within the family, are less trustful of the world beyond the family boundaries. Centrifugal (CF) family members, on the other hand, seeking gratification from beyond the confines of the family, often trust activities and relationships outside the family unit more than those within it" (1993, 75). In systems theory, family health is found in a balance of the two styles: "Representing the clinical and empirical findings that healthy families show a flexible and blended family style, such that they can adapt stylistic behavior as developmental, individual, and family needs change over time.

At the most dysfunctional end of the competence dimension are seen the most extreme and inflexible family styles" (77).

From this description, the centripetal extreme fits the *contained* end where the self implodes, cutting off contact from the outside. In contrast, the centrifugal extreme fits the *dispersed* end where the self spins away from its center into explosive fragmentation. A person's place can be depicted on a curvilinear graph where too small a place for the self, the contained self, or too large a place for the self, the dispersed self, becomes lethal. Life is not found on any fixed point on the continuum but is unfolded in the dance that balances both ends of the continuum. Here it is a linear graph where most flexibility in balancing opposites affords optimal health.

The two ways of death continuum sets the perimeters of countless ways of being in the world. As a result, *preparing a place* counseling approaches will need to vary according to the location of the person or group of persons on the continuum. There is no one formula of good spiritual care and therapy. The optimal balance between the two ends of the self-in-the-world continuum will vary from person to person, from family to family, and from time to time.

The *contained self* fits what the existentialists have called finitude's despair: "Too much finitude, too much limitation by the body and the behaviors of the person in the real world, and not enough freedom of the inner self, of inner symbolic possibility...depressive psychosis as a bogging down in the demands of others—family, job, the narrow horizon of daily duties" (Becker, 1973, 78). The contained self fits with the older psychoanalytic concept of the neurotic character, the person afflicted by chronic anxiety and inner conflict, inhibited in self-expression and social interaction. Growth approaches and human potential therapies fit a liberation model of therapy designed to release a person from being boxed in. In Gestalt therapy health is defined as a continuous process of creative adjustments: "the ever-renewed transition between novelty and routine, resulting in assimilation and growth" (Perls, Hefferline & Goodman, 1951, 230-231). It is the picture of either flowing or stagnant waters that signals the conditions of life or death. Virginia Satir sees life in a person when "there is an integration, a flowing, an aliveness, an openness, and what I call a juiciness..." (1972, 74). In a process conception of therapy, Carl Rogers portrays seven successive stages of growth "by which the individual changes from fixity to flowingness, from a point nearer the rigid end of the continuum to a point nearer the "in motion" end of the continuum" (1961, 132). The culmination of therapy is reached when "the person becomes a unity of flow, of motion. He [sic] has changed. But what seems most significant, he has become an integrated process of changingness" (1961, 132, 158).

In contrast, the *dispersed self* suffers from too much movement, too much possibility. Beavers's (1990) research studies show that while centripetal families exhibit more internalizing disorders such as anxiety and depression, centrifugal families exhibit more externalizing disorders such as acting out and aggressive behavior. The madness of psychotic disorientation in a Tom shows an example of the self losing its grounding in the world and being dispersed in fragmentation. In this instance, institutionalization became one way to contain the self and provide a safe place.

There are many less extreme examples of caring for those on the dispersed side of the continuum. Religious counseling often seeks to bring structure to a disordered world where people can get lost. Moral guidance has been part of the traditional task of the religious community in orientating the person to a world of values and meanings. Don Browning emphasizes the moral context of pastoral care: "Pastoral care must first give a person a structure, a character, an identity, a religiocultural value system out of which to live" (1976, 103). Rather than a moralistic focus on what the person is to do or not to do, therapeutic care moralizes by preparing a place of orientation in the world out of which to live. Crisis counseling is another example where a more directive, structured approach is the appropriate response to the threat of being dispersed by disorienting stress and overwhelming change.

Reality therapy has been successful with people who suffer from the disorder of chaotic social environments and/or criminal life styles. The displacement I encountered at a halfway house for women parolees was largely systemic. The people were women, parolees, poor, with deprived and often abusive family and social backgrounds, most of them members of visible minorities: a toxic cocktail of damaging and stigmatizing variables. The ministry of preparing a place became systemic: spiritual care through community outreach with prison visiting programs, residential care centers, and re-entry care packages consisting of educational programs and employment supports.

Family therapy defines the person's place in the context of significant others. *Marriage and family therapy* prepares a place by achieving a balance between building closer relationships and defining the self as distinct from these relationships. Family therapy maps the dense geography of the ties that bind, analyzes scripts of dominant family narratives and legacies, and explores the dark holes of emotional cut-offs. *Contextual therapy* locates itself in the "in-between" territories of "give and take," in the covenants of relational ethics articulated in the delicate balances between loyalties to others and entitlements for the self, and works to build the bonds of mutual trustworthiness.

The various styles of the therapies, despite the many differences, share the common theme of the human need for a place. The human condition presents a constant challenge to our place in life, forever shifting the precarious balance between being in and out of place in the world. Migration narratives of the search for a place script sacred stories and provide the horizons for the practice of care in preparing a place.

CHAPTER 3

◈ Cross-Spiritual Therapy

THIS CHAPTER WILL EXPLORE spirituality as infinitely multiple and uniquely personal. As a personal perspective on, and way of living the meaning of, one's life, spirituality becomes a pluralistic and idiosyncratic experience. Spirituality is not predicated by religious dogma and thus is not constricted to or prescribed by a particular faith community. Even though a person's religious affiliation or background will likely be a contributing factor in shaping his or her spiritual outlook, each person will configure out of life's many influences a spirituality profoundly one's own. This view of spirituality carries the assumption that spiritual care providers cannot start with certainties. As caregivers we cannot assume that such givens as a person's religion or lack of it, family of origin history, personality typology or diagnostic profile reveal that person's spirituality. Nor can we presume that we have the answers that will fit this particular life. Spiritual care is, therefore, primarily a practice of listening and learning to relate to another's personal sense of his or her special place in the world and the larger universe.

Varieties of Spirituality

The century-old William James classic, The Varieties of Religious Experience (1902), may well be one of the most relevant texts in today's search to address therapy to spiritual concerns. Rather than objectifying and generalizing religion in its creeds and practices, James focuses on religion as the passionate human striving for deliverance and unification of the self. Anticipating modern ethnographic methodology, Varieties follows a subjectivist and existential approach on pages soaked in extreme, if not sick, religious experiences. With a single focus on religious experience, James discovered wide diversity, which he sorted into typologies and polarities such as healthy- and morbid-minded, tough- and tender-minded. These categories are not pure types to be kept separate, but can coexist in collusive patterns of interaction. Nor can their respective spiritual value or contribution to health be measured or ranked. According to James, if any functional primacy is to be accorded to a particular type of religious experience, it belongs to the sick soul. The prominence of the sick soul, with its accompanying feelings of insecurity, condemnation and fear, is that it drives the soul beyond itself in a desperate search to complete itself.

The metaphor of a soul yearning to connect with its home base has long been at the core of conceptualizing human spirituality. As stated by William James, in religious sentiment the visible world is embedded in an invisible spiritual universe from which human life derives its chief meaning and purpose. In a similar vein, existential theologian Paul Tillich (1957) expressed the essence of religion in the concept of a person's *ultimate concern*, which is further defined as the soul's *passion for the infinite*. Ultimate concerns also stand out in the topographical metaphor of *Theological Worlds* where Paul Jones (1989) described spiritual striving in a theological world constituted by an *obsessio* (dilemma) attuned to a contrasting *epiphania* (resolution). There are diverse theological worlds and the "rhythm" in each is found in the interplay between the respective poles of *obsessio* and *epiphania*. A variety of spiritualities thus emerges in polar dyads: Separation and Reunion, Conflict and Vindication, Emptiness and Fulfillment, Condemnation and Forgiveness, and Suffering and Endurance.

This variety of theological worlds reflects the sweeping scope in current definitions of spirituality where the spiritual quest covers vast territory: for unity and reconciliation, for acceptance and love, for attainment of one's potential, for fulfillment of one's true vocation, for ultimate meaning and transcendence, for connection and community, for the courage to be and to endure. Spiritual care marks the kind of therapy that is less directed by the concerns of every-day living, significant as these may be, than by the struggles of the soul. The practice of spiritual care requires the openness and curiosity of a William James in savoring the varieties of spiritual experiences. Rather than being confined to one theoretically dominant or personally preferred perspective, caregivers need multiple perspectives to join with people as they share their spiritual experiences and concerns. A cross-spiritual spectrum facilitates greater flexibility in identifying core questions that are being raised as well as locating the particular theological world in which these questions reside.

This chapter outlines three distinctive spiritualities that have been prominent in the history and practice of spiritual care. In exploring the distinctive features of different spiritual experiences, the history and language of religion, spirituality, and psychology meet in constructing a multi-spiritual spectrum. For spiritual care to be inclusive, it needs an orienting framework that can accommodate the variety of spiritual experiences encountered in clinical practice. The proposed outline of three distinctive spiritual territories is an inclusive but not comprehensive approach. No map is sufficiently stretched and multicolored to encompass the vastness and diversity of spiritual experiences. Another caveat is to note that these three territories are not demarcated by closed boundaries. Different spiritual perspectives are not mutually exclusive. Yet in the counseling situation one perspective is often dominant. While a person may hold dual citizenship, even maintain a foothold in several theological worlds, primary residence will probably be in one of those worlds.

Three Perspectives

Multiple perspectives in spirituality invite a flexible and differential approach in spiritual care. The chapter outlines three perspectives defined respectively by the common terms: *grace, growth,* and *resilience.* Obviously, each perspective in this triad represents universal and inclusive features of spirituality. At the same time, each perspective is unique, bounded by its own historical context and spiritual meanings. The three perspectives are markedly distinct and can be arranged in historical sequence, tracing the emergence of a variety of meaning worlds in Western society:

- The perspective of the *grace of God* is prominent in the world of religion. The doctrine of the triumph of God's grace over human failures stirred both religious sentiments and ecclesiastical turmoil toward the end of the Middle Ages. The centrality of *sola gratia* then reached beyond the Protestant Reformation to a broad ecumenical confession. For many, grace is also present in a non-religious spirituality through the experience of grateful surprise. It is the grace that comes in discontinuous change, outside human control or choice. This grace exists in the bright moments when, in spite of everything, life is good and forgiving.

- The *perspective of growth* of the self is highlighted in the world of psychology, in the emphasis on *human potential* found in self-actualizing humanistic psychology since the 1960s. The psychoanalytic school of Self Psychology raised an additional growth emphasis in the 1970s. Its developmental approach has gained increasing prominence as a practice that normalizes and supports perpetual narcissistic strivings towards a cohesive self. Another major psychology that ascended in the 1970s, family systems theory, places the elusive goal of *self-differentiation* at the very core in the evolving family life cycle—the ability to both leave and come home again.

- The *perspective of resilience* of the human spirit spans a broad, interdisciplinary spectrum in the world of the social sciences. Resilience embraces the human struggle to manage and survive the many trials and traumas of life. It is set against the backdrop of violence-ridden societies and stress-saturated day-to-day lives leading to anxiety-disordered personal worlds. Due to persistent lobbying by veterans' groups, the 1980 edition of the American Psychiatric Association's *Diagnostic and Statistical Manual of Mental Disorders* (DSM-III) included "Posttraumatic Stress Disorder" as a discrete diagnostic category. Initially related to the debilitating effects of the Vietnam War, the diagnosis is presently stretched to include the potentially devastating impact of poverty, child abuse, loss of a loved one, discrimination, domestic violence, natural disasters, traffic accidents, couple infidelity, physical disabilities and many other traumatizing experiences. Resilience, the bright sparkle in the darkness of despair, highlights the intrinsic penchant of the human spirit to find hope in the future and a path through the traumas of life.

The Perspective of Grace

The perspective of grace is prominent in many of the case studies recounted in William James recounts in *Varieties*. The chapter on *the sick soul* is rooted in James's own history of extreme depression culminating in a frightful panic attack. Assuming that James voiced the experience through an imaginary correspondent from France (see Wulff, 1991, 472; Erikson, 1968, 152), he recounts the moment of dread "when suddenly there fell upon me without any warning, just as if it came out of the darkness, a horrible fear of my own existence. Simultaneously there arose in my mind the image of an epileptic patient whom I had seen in the asylum, a black-haired youth with greenish skin, entirely idiotic... moving nothing but his black eyes and looking absolutely non-human. This image and my fear entered into a species of combination with each other. That shape am I, I felt, potentially." James adds that "the fear was so invasive and powerful that if I had not clung to scripture-texts like 'The eternal God is my refuge,' etc., 'Come unto me, all ye that labor and are heavy-laden,' etc., 'I am the resurrection and the life,' etc., I think I should have grown really insane" (1960, 135, 136).

The personal narratives in *Varieties*, many composed from a Christian persuasion, come from troubled souls in desperate search for salvation. Their dominant *theological world* is built on the dialectic of condemnation and forgiveness. The case studies generally paint condemnation as an overwhelming sense of sin and guilt with resulting feelings of utter helplessness. James describes this as the dilemma of *the divided self*: the sense that there is an evil inner core that separates us from what we aspire to, and that "we must lose the one before we can participate in the other" (140).

James marks this existential dread as the necessary passage to new life. He speaks for a religion of deliverance: "the man [sic] must die to an unreal life before he can be born into the real life" (139). Despair sets the stage for the experience of grace. Grace is signaled by the liberating moment when guilt dissolves into the assurance of free forgiveness. James cites a classic case example rooted in Reformation theology through the testimony of Martin Luther, who after the moment of grace, exhibited at times an almost callous disregard for sin:

> "When I was a monk," he [Luther] says, "I thought that I was utterly cast away, if at any time I felt the lust of the flesh: that is to say, if I felt any evil motion, fleshly lust, wrath, hatred, or envy against any brother, I assayed many ways to help to quiet my conscience, but it would not be; for the concupiscence and lust of my flesh did always return, so that I could not rest, but was continually

vexed with these thoughts: This or that sin thou hast committed: thou art infected with envy, with impatience, and such other sins: therefore thou art entered into this holy order in vain, and all thy good works are unprofitable. But if then I had rightly understood these sentences of Paul: 'The flesh lusteth contrary to the Spirit, and the Spirit contrary to the flesh; and these two are one against another, so that ye cannot do the things that ye would do,' I should not have so miserably tormented myself, but should have though and said to myself, as now commonly I do, 'Martin, thou shalt not be utterly be without sin, for thou hast flesh; thou shalt therefore feel the battle thereof.'" (113)

This radical, unconventional view of the all-sufficiency of grace without further requirements or expectations is hard to maintain in the social and moral structure of a religious community. Marcus Borg, born and raised a Lutheran, reflects how for many Lutherans the initial emphasis on *grace* tended to shift to *faith* as the new requirement: "*Faith* (most often understood as *belief*) is what God required, and by a lack of faith/belief one risked the peril of eternal punishment" (Borg, 1994, 79). This may explain the common theme in spiritual narratives that grace appears as a surprise in unlikely places often outside the religious community. Some even designate grace as the marker that distinguishes spirituality from religion. In a recent study of life-transforming experiences, a woman reports: "Eventually, as a Christian, I came to accept who I was, that God loves me. The difference between religion and spirituality, in my mind, is that in any church you go to what you hear is: 'God loves you if...God loves you if you give ten percent; God loves you if you are straight, not gay; God loves you if you don't believe in abortion; God loves if.' To me, after that experience, spirituality is: God loves me, period, unconditionally and no ifs. It's there. I can tap into it. It's for me" (Miller & C'de Baca, 2001, 137).

Although Freud was not a friend of the world of religion, his psychology parallels the religious version of the dilemma of a divided self. Psychoanalytic theory sees the self divided between the unconscious and the conscious. The unconscious represents the biological, antisocial forces of the instincts that crave for instant gratification. Consciousness represents a higher level of mental awareness attuned to social sensitivity and a moral order. The split between the conscious and the unconscious is initially experienced as dividing the self into two contrary forces locked in adversarial tension. Repression is the line of defense that cuts the self into two incompatible territories to be kept apart.

This psychoanalytic perspective readily translates into the language of Jewish-Christian religion. For Freud the story of the fall into sin originates in the archaic family drama of the oedipal conflict. Original sin stems from the act of transgressing into the forbidden territory of desiring what belongs to the father. This sin evokes the father's anger and the child's guilt and fear of terminal punishment. The resolution to this dilemma is to be pursued in the search for the unification of the self. For Freud this is achieved through exploring one's unconscious world in the presence of an accepting, non-judging analyst. The hope is that the process of self-examination in free association and rational interpretation will lead to a unified self in accepting and owning the duplicity implicit in being human.

The Perspective of Growth

Like William James's *Varieties of Religious Experience*, William Miller's and Janet C'de Baca's book, *Quantum Change: When Epiphanies and Sudden Insights Transform Ordinary Lives* (2001), was published at the start of a new century. Though a century apart, the two books parallel each other in a subjective research approach to studying life-changing spiritual experiences. Where the hundred years have made a difference is that the varieties have become more diverse, reflecting contemporary shifts in spirituality.

In current psychoanalytic practice, self psychology discovered that fewer clients demonstrate the classic neurotic struggle with inhibitions and guilt (Gabbard, 1990, 37-42). In contrast, many contemporary clients are troubled by chronic feelings of low self-worth and conflicted by their emotional dependence on unflagging support and admiration (Kohut, 1977). These "narcissistic" strivings originate in a pre-oedipal stage of human development, located in the neediness of the small child for constant affirmation and reassurance from the parent. Deficits in attending to a child's needs for acknowledgement leave a legacy of enduring pain of being left empty and insecure in the world. The spiritual impetus is towards restoration and fulfillment of the self in overcoming these nurturing deficits from the past.

Self psychology has become increasingly prominent in the practice of spiritual care. There is ample evidence that current religious experiences are no longer primarily defined by guilt and the search for forgiveness. Pastoral theologian Donald Capps, in his book *The Depleted Self: Sin in a Narcissistic Age* (1993), refutes the damning connotations of narcissism in this empathic description of the current dominant spiritual malaise: "We seem chronically depleted, doubtful of our worth, emotionally hungry, and highly attuned and sensitive to shame. Moments of elation and satisfaction cannot be enjoyed or even trusted because we know that soon the bubble will burst, the joy will dissipate, and the life will go out of us, leaving us, once again, feeling empty and depleted" (36).

Miller and C'de Baca include personal narratives that poignantly illustrate the spirituality of growth. *A Mirror and Two Roses* (57-60), for example, identifies three critical events in the writer's life. It started when an old friend crossed his path, looked at him and said: "You're fat!" Inwardly he reacted with indignation: "How dare you tell me that? I'm not fat! Who are you to tell me that?" The second event came after a night of solitary drinking in a hotel room on a New Year's Eve. The next morning, ready to check out, he looked in the mirror:

"I didn't recognize what I saw. There was a real split, I guess, between my inner self and the self that the outside world could see. I didn't like what I saw. I saw a fat person…I didn't see a healthy person. I didn't see a happy person." This mirror image shook him in a profound way. He recounts the moment that he thought: "You're a smart person. What can you do to make yourself feel better?" He continues: "I had never exercised regularly, but I started walking every day. Then I began running. After a year I was still at it, running six miles at least twice a week. I also started eating healthier foods, and it worked. I slimmed down, and people noticed and complimented me. I stopped drinking heavily. During the same time I began feeling more confident and taking initiative in the business where I worked. My ideas were successful for the company, and within the year they had doubled my salary. I moved to a nicer apartment and bought a new car."

Similar to the spirituality of grace, there is in this story of personal transformation a *divided self*, but of a different kind. In the perspective of grace an inward division is drawn between a bad inner nature and the good intentions of the self. In the perspective of growth, the division is between one's awareness of inner strength and the outside world's inability to see that strength. The author states the dilemma: "There was a real split, I guess, between my inner self and the self that the outside world could see."

The core metaphor of the story is the mirror. Initially his life reflected a flawed human image to others. In the second event in the hotel room, he gets a mirror glimpse of himself as others see him: "I didn't see a healthy person. I didn't see a happy person." This motivated him to shape up his appearance and performance. With this new and real mirror image of himself, he found that "people noticed and complimented me." The writer does not describe his personal transformation as a religious conversion, saying: "It wasn't really a religious thing, like people who are born again. I'm not a religious person."

For others, the experience of becoming who you really are marks of the presence of God experienced as an act of grace. In her story notably titled *Awakening* (61-65) a woman reflects on the moment of a radical shift in her awareness: "Then one day I suddenly felt a sense of presence about myself that I had never felt before. I knew that the way I was living was not right—that there was more, and most that there was more to me. I had been living a part of myself, but a part that was a hazy sort of person who moved through life and did things well, without a strong awareness or consciousness. That one day, I just became very aware of this. I just felt this presence of a real self within me." That day marked her entry into a larger world where she felt her life connecting with God: "I know that there is something I'm destined to do, that there is a greater purpose for me. That doesn't mean I am going to move the earth or do something profound, but it is profound in the sense that I have found my place on earth. I have made that connection with God. I'm just a person walking around here on earth. God is within me, and I have to pay more attention to the godliness that is really truly me. There's something specific that I'm here for." Her place in the world has become a sacred place where she is connected with her true objectives and can discern God's presence within her and follow her vocation in life.

The Perspective of Resilience

Though a perennial human quality, resilience is a relatively new perspective in the field of therapy. Much of the clinical literature has focused on individual pathology and family dysfunction to be countered by clever therapeutic strategies designed to overcome client difficulties and resistance. Current collaborative therapies emphasize a shift in perspective from deficits to resources, from damage to challenge. Family therapist Froma Walsh (1993, 1998) stresses that "we need to understand how families can survive and regenerate even in the midst of overwhelming stress, adversity, or life-altering transition" (1993, 55). Others (Wolin & Wolin, 1993) have studied how some people in hostile environments and circumstances not only survived but actually gained in inner strength and ingenuity.

Miller and C'de Baca recount a narrative that serves well in illustrating the perspective of resilience. The story, which displays the human agility of bouncing back from the traumas and trials of life, is appropriately titled *Trampoline* (118-123). Its author recounts how as a young gymnastics trampoline teacher he inadvertently landed on his head after demonstrating a double back flip. He damaged his spinal cord and faced the prospect of being paralyzed from the neck down: "In a split second, I went from being a very, very active person—one who needed twenty-eight hours a day to get everything done and running full blast driving here and there and going everywhere all the time—to just not being able to move." The personal narrative is interspersed with the following resilience signals:

- I began thinking "What are my options now?"

- It was about a week afterward that I first really put it into words when I was talking with one of the nurses, that it was like I was starting my life all over again, being born all over again, except this time my mind was fully developed and I'd be learning to live all over again.

- Everything, virtually everything, that I had been doing in my life, I was going to have to put on the back bookshelf of my mind and be a resource to draw from for problem solving later on in life.

- Just start anew and take it one step at a time. The first ones are going to be small, baby steps, and than maybe some larger ones, and then maybe a break through or bigger steps, or maybe a step backward.

- My spiritual grounding was very helpful. I knew that there was a bigger picture...God would use it in some way that I had no idea of at that time. I knew that there was a plan for this in some way, and it would turn out to be for the best.

- The slowing down of my lifestyle allowed me to see a lot more of the beauty in the world, just to take time to see and to analyze it. To see people and not judge them on a quick first impression, not judge them for what they do right then, but to see them more compassionately in a longer-term picture. It makes for a whole lot nicer world.

- One of my little hobbies is writing poems.

- I really try to be positive, see the positive side of anything that's going on. My spirituality is deeper and more enhanced.

The above profile illustrates the dynamics of a resilient spirit. The pieces shape a collage of a unique response to suffering. The man is not overwhelmed by feelings of despair and resentment, rather he experiences defiant hope and steady endurance. Endurance in resilience is not just a passive quality but can generate protest and social action. In the context of physical and sexual violence in families or abuse of power in society, resilience often is the core of the narratives of survival and resistance. Poling cites courageous stories of women's active resilience in response to abuse and points to Jesus's resistance to abusive powers: "For many resilient spirits through the ages, Jesus has been an inspiring figure of hope in the midst of evil" (1991, 35). Others have identified resilience as the outstanding feature in Jewish spirituality (Wolin, 1999).

Human resilience is often found in unlikely places such as chronic care facilities. O'Connor and Meakes (2001) studied forgiveness and resentment among people with a major disability that permanently confines them to institutional care, their restrictions both demonstrated and defied by a wheelchair. Surprisingly their research found that forgiveness is high and resentment is low (297-311). Resilience comes across as a spirituality of optimism—that there is a way through the obstacles of life. While grace is inspired by a power larger than the self, and growth is supported by the promise of the real self, the spirituality of resilience is contextual and practiced in community. Developmentally it draws on adult functions of planning, collaborating, and problem-solving. God is not so much a parent, rescuing the child from its miseries in the world, as a faithful companion and a partner in the daily tasks of assessing and challenging the adversities of life.

Applications

Following William James, this chapter has focused on the varieties of spiritual orientation. The three spiritualities I have articulated generate case studies of difference and root the thesis that spiritual care requires a multiperspectival approach. Table 3.1 condenses the material here by highlighting the points of differentiation. Differentiation is crucial in the process of joining

with people as they share their spiritual experiences. The table does not pretend
to outline the nature of spirituality. It does not propose a tripartite structural theory of spirituality. The focus, rather, is on the practice of spiritual care. Perspectives pave the pathways that lead to the various theological worlds that
map people's spiritual experiences. Caregivers often sense that their own theological world charts foreign territory for others but that a different perspective
clears common ground. Likewise for counselors, a specific therapy model may
feel awkward in a particular client situation, demonstrating the need for an
inclusive therapy framework that matches person and method, context and
approach. Solution-focused therapy may fit a resilience situation but is offensive to a "sick soul" seeking grace.

Table 3.1   Three Spiritual Perspectives

Perspectives	Grace	Growth	Resilience
Theological Dialectic	condemnation & forgiveness	emptiness & fulfillment	suffering & endurance
Psychosocial Dynamic	guilt & acceptance	shame & confirmation	inferiority & resources
Psychoanalytic	oedipal	pre-oedipal	post-oedipal
Pathologic	sick soul	depleted self	discouraged spirit
Pathogenic	sin	deficit	damage
God Image	father	mother	companion
Therapeutic	representative	reflective	reconstructive

Therapy models define themselves by their *modus operandi* with their respective styles of communication. Varieties in spiritual experience require diversity
in communication, a multi-channel transmission. Therapeutic communication is not of one piece but comes in different shapes as it seeks to accomplish
different ends. Chapter 5 links various therapeutic styles of communication to
three different roles in spiritual care: *representative, reflective, and reconstructive.*
These three categories correspond to the three spiritualities of grace, growth,
and resilience. The representative role focuses on the counselor who brings an
authoritative and trustworthy message. The descriptions of the "sick soul" in
Varieties emphasize the role of sacred scriptures and the guidance of mentors in
a shared context. The representative style communicates assurance for those
seeking grace and acceptance. The reflective role does not appeal to external
truth claims but celebrates the person's special worth through a respectful

attending and mirroring presence. This style enhances deeply personal encounters with those seeking growth and confirmation. The reconstructive role in communication is collaborating with others in the meaning-making and problem-solving process of day-to-day living, based on the belief that people are resilient, viewing life and challenging its hardships with steady defiance and hope.

A multi-perspectival approach makes spiritual care a variant of cross-cultural counseling (Augsburger, 1986): the readiness and ability to meet people on their own territory, in the course of their own journey. Such encounters induce a spirit of wonder and curiosity in the caregiver. As two clinicians describe their experience of a multi-spiritual approach in therapy: "We have been least successful when we felt that a prior understanding, whether from religious studies or personal experience, has given us a head start in comprehending....The skills most helpful for opening therapy to the spiritual and religious domains have been those for preparing our own selves to meet someone not yet known" (Griffith & Griffith, 2002, 26, 27).

PART TWO

Essentials
of
Caring

CHAPTER 4

▧ What to Know:
Therapeutic Models

THE QUESTION "WHAT IS THE PROBLEM?" signals the beginning of the therapy process, setting the stage for the development of the helping relationship and the emerging therapeutic strategy. Rather than saying the word "problem" aloud, most initial helping interviews soften the question to a polite, "What brings you here?" or "How can I be of help?" Questions that pursue the problem ("Can you tell me a bit more about that?") and probe its impact ("How did that feel?" or "What was your wife's reaction?") structure the helping plan. On a more personal level, the process of telling, hearing and exploring the problem determines the depth and emotional connection in the emerging helping alliance.

With so much at stake, the problem easily becomes a center of anxiety. The person with "the problem" may worry whether in the therapist's assessment the problem is "good enough" to gain attention and warrant therapy. Worse, the problem may be "bad enough" to repel rather than engage helpers. The therapist too has reason to worry in the initial interview. The "presenting problem" is the place of mutual introductions: a place where the person seeking help and the person offering help present themselves to each other. Not only the client but also the counselor is assessed. In the "presenting problem" the client assesses the level of the therapist's clinical understanding and personal caring. The therapist may experience the "presenting problem" as the test to check his or her competence. Thus, a "sticky" problem is passed on from client to therapist, potentially resulting into a joint stuckness.

In the triangle of client, therapist and presenting problem, the problem often becomes the midwife in the evolving therapeutic alliance:

1. The *presenting* problem may be primarily the stage for client and therapist to become *present* to each other. When asked in supervision, therapists often need to pause and think hard to remember their clients' initial presenting problem. The *problem* served as an initiation ritual in the formation of the helping relationship, only to become background to other situations to emerge as foreground figure.

2. The presenting problem may recede to the background in the process of developing a helping plan. Effective therapy rightly differentiates between life's difficulties and the process by which these difficulties become prob-

lems. The therapist coaches and collaborates with the client to revise a global or terminal problem-definition, amending it to a more workable, therapy-friendly formulation.

On the other hand, in cases where the presenting problem resists all attempts at editorial revisions, the problem increasingly asserts its dominant position in the counseling triangle. An intractable presenting problem thus tends to contaminate the helping relationship. For the therapist the problem can become the client: the client *is* rather than *has* a problem. In parallel fashion for the client, the problem can become the therapist. Such a scenario follows a *musical chairs* triangle with the interchanging roles of victim, persecutor and rescuer (Karpman, 1968). The client initially presents as victim of the problem as the persecutor, recruiting the therapist as rescuer. When the problem stubbornly persists, despite the therapist's best efforts, the therapist shifts to the role of victim persecuted by a demanding or a so-called "resistant" client, while the client may well feel persecuted by an incompetent or unsympathetic therapist.

Having highlighted the crucial role of the presenting problem in the evolving therapeutic relationship, this chapter will focus on the connection between the presenting problem and the model of therapy used to understand the problem. A therapy model functions as a medium of interpretation or coding system, linking a problem definition to a problem resolution in a therapeutic strategy. How a particular problem is understood depends on the perspective of any given school of therapy. This makes the presenting problem the criterion in differentiating the various approaches among the schools of psychotherapy. The following brief history of the schools of therapy will illustrate shifts in defining and locating the "problem" in the helping process.

Mapping the Therapies

Conventional psychoanalytic therapies often appear interested not so much in solving as in interpreting patient problems. Rather than alleviate the problem, therapy is to lay bare its roots and deeper meanings. Problems in the present serve as surface symptoms that call for in-depth analysis to uncover the "real" problem with its origins in the past. This *extrinsic problem definition* addresses the root causes of the presenting problem and focuses on the question, "Why is there a problem?"

Behavior therapy and family therapy, though distinct therapy systems, reacted against this psychodynamic approach. Both therapies emphasized solving the problem as presented in the "here and now." This *intrinsic problem definition* equates solving the problem with eliminating the problem as presented by the client. The question does not focus on *why* but rather on "*what* is the problem?" This problem-focused position stands out in strategic family therapy and is succinctly articulated in the title of Jay Haley's 1976 book, *Problem-*

Solving Therapy. In a book published twenty years later, Haley has not wavered in his conviction that:

> Therapists should be taught that the most immediate decision when therapy begins, a decision that reflects their general orientation, is whether to focus on the problem presented ... If their therapist focuses on the presenting symptom, clients consider themselves understood. If the therapist focuses on what is behind the symptom—or above it or below it, in the roots—clients will have to be patient until the therapist gets around to what they are paying their money to have changed. (1996, 94)

In spite of this anti-psychodynamic polemic, both early family and behavioral therapies share the same *objectivistic* presuppositions as espoused in psychoanalytic theories. This philosophy of realism asserts that psychological processes can be objectively observed and articulated in scientific theory. Psychoanalytic, behavioral and family systems all agreed that there is a "scientifically correct" way of doing therapy but disagreed in their respective competitive claims of theoretical and clinical superiority.

Objectivist therapies with an extrinsic problem definition offer a vision of normative reality intended to enlighten, inspire or direct a person's way of being in the world. Apart from the teachers of psychoanalytic therapies (from Freud to Kohut), this approach includes many other therapies popular in spiritual care and in the literature of pastoral counseling: analytic psychology (Jung), transactional analysis (Berne), and natural systems family theory (Bowen), to mention a few. Such objectivist belief and therapy systems are challenged by the *subjectivist* presuppositions of phenomenological theories that gained prominence in the 1960s. Subjectivism stresses a reality relative to personal experience. Existential philosophies, enhanced by the clinical practice of client-centered therapy, question privileged professional knowledge presumed in the more authoritative, proclamatory therapies. From the experiential perspective, therapy seeks to be person-centered rather than centered in theory, reality or truth claims.

A similar subjectivist shift impacted the objectivist therapies with the "intrinsic problem" focus. In the 1970s, both behavior therapy and family system therapies were challenged by the cognitive therapies. The theory of *constructivism*, eloquently articulated by the Mental Research Institute (MRI) at Palo Alto, became highly influential in family therapy. It addressed the principles of problem formation and resolution as mental processes that construct subjective realities (Watzlawick, Weakland & Fisch, 1974). Following that line, the therapy of realism increasingly became a therapy of interpretation. The focus shifted from the problem "as presented" to the problem "as constructed" in its manifold personal meanings and relational functions.

Solution-focused therapy in the 1980s targeted the solution rather than the problem. This has a radical implication for the helping relationship. Gone is the

Figure 4.1   Therapeutic Strategies Map

Objectivist Problem Resolution

Behavior Therapies

Strategic / Structural
Family Therapies

Psychoanalytic Theories

Analytic Psychology

Natural Systems Family Theory

Religious Therapy Systems

Psychoeducational Therapy

MRI

Intrinsic   **Extrinsic**

Problem Definition   **Problem Definition**

Solution-Focused
Therapy

Narrative / Constructivist
Therapies

Humanistic / Existential Theories

Experiential Family Therapy

Person-Centered Therapies

Collaborative Language
Therapy Systems

Subjectivist Problem Resolution

Problem Definition

intrinsic
- solving the problem is eliminating the problem
- focus on "*what* is the problem?"

extrinsic
- addressing the root causes of the problem
- focus on "*why* have the problem?"

Problem Resolution

objectivist
- objective theory / truth focused
- reality as given and to be discovered

subjectivist
- subjective interpretation focused
- reality as personally and socially constructed

task division by which the client owns the problem and the therapist the solution. Now the client is credited for having the potential to generate not only the
problem but also its solution. Current brief therapies have matched the emphasis on the solution-generating abilities of the client with declining attention for
the problem. Some have even cut the problem-definition/solution connection
by saying that "you do not need to know what the problem is in order to solve
it," and "the solution is not necessarily related to the problem" (deShazer, 1991,
xii).

Success in the conventional objectivist therapies, whether oriented toward
insight or action, is mediated through the competence of a therapist or counselor who knows, and knows what to do. In contrast, current postmodern
approaches, ranging from *solution-focused* to *constructivist/narrative* therapies, cultivate a therapeutic stance of uncertainty. Curiosity joins therapist and client in
meaning-generating conversations toward collaboratively defined therapeutic
goals.

A note of caution: diagrams like Figure 4.1 are tools of simplification that
reduce complex realities to categories that can be grasped and imagined as distinct entities. Major schools of therapy initially arose as exclusive, orthodox
belief systems emphasizing their uniqueness and distinctiveness. Boundaries
have since become more fluid. The various therapies begin to sound ecumenical in articulating not only their differences but also points of connection, often
advocating the advantages of integration and cooperation in clinical practice.
By distinguishing and discriminating between the major models of caring in
clinical education programs, we seek, as one major text states, "to respect the
search for common principles in theory or practice while continuing to appreciate and highlight the different perspectives each model or school of therapy
exemplifies" (Gurman & Messer, 1995, 2).

A Case Example

The following verbatim account of a first counseling interview illustrates the various possibilities in defining and addressing a presenting
problem:

Therapist: What brings you here for therapy?
  Client: I have a fear of crossing bridges.

Therapist: Do you have any other fears or difficulties?
  Client: Only the complications arising from my fear of bridges.

Therapist: In what way has it affected your life?
  Client: I had to quit an excellent job because I had to cross a long
          bridge.

> Therapist: Tell me, how long have you had this problem?
>
> Client: Oh, about four years, I'd say. It just happened suddenly. I was coming home from work and the bridge was awfully slow. I just suddenly panicked for no reason at all. I mean, nothing like this had ever happened to me before. I had a feeling that the bridge would cave in.
>
> Therapist: You said that you were coming home from work. Had anything happened at work?
>
> Client: Nothing unusual.
>
> Therapist: Were you happy at your work?
>
> Client: Sure! Huh! I was even due for promotion to become a supervisor. I would have had more than fifty people working under me.
>
> Therapist: How did you feel about the added responsibility? Did you feel you were up to it?
>
> Client: Gee! My wife was expecting our first kid. We both welcomed the extra money.
>
> Therapist: So round about the time that you were about to become a father, you were to be promoted to supervisor. You'd be a daddy at home and also big daddy at work. And this was when you began to panic on the bridge, and I guess you never did wind up as a supervisor.

I have adapted this example from an actual case reported by the well-known early behavior therapist, Arnold Lazarus (1971, 36-38). He entitled his book *Behavior Therapy & Beyond* to illustrate from his own clinical practice that some problems demand procedures that go beyond conventional behavior therapy. In his discussion of the bridge phobia, Lazarus contends that a "behaviorist" approach unduly limits therapy to the bridge as the sole stimulus event triggering the anxiety response. He asks: "Did not his bridge phobia serve the function of preventing the full impact of his own uncertainties and shortcomings vis-à-vis his work, competence, obligations, and achievements?" In this case, Lazarus worked with a *family-of-origin* approach, "a history in which the patient, the youngest of five siblings, tended to accept his mother's evaluation that, unlike his brilliant older brothers, he would never amount to anything" (38).

The "bridge phobia" provides fertile grounds for extrinsic problem definitions by the schools of objectivism. *Object relations* theory may see the bridge as the trigger for separation/abandonment anxiety, a bridge about to collapse as it strains to span the expanding distance between the internalized "baby" and "daddy's" adult responsibilities. Jungian therapy may focus on archetypal images: the water as the unconscious and the bridge as a symbol of transition to unknown shores. Bowen's natural systems theory may address the anxiety as coming from the family of origin's emotional system in resisting the "baby" of the family becoming a self-differentiated adult.

Intrinsic problem-resolutions proposed by the objectivist schools of therapy will be likewise manifold. A paradoxical intervention in strategic therapy might have the client explore a map for locating long bridges within driving distance, with the instruction to cross bridges at least twice each day for a week and have at least one panic attack daily. The subjectivist approach of narrative therapy could externalize the bridge phobia as a place where the client experiences himself as "stretched to the limit" or "out of his depth," and invite other "stories of panic" for finding exceptions and differences. Hermeneutical/conversational therapy would resist the language of phobias or other assorted pathologies, while engaging in meaning-making dialogue, reflecting on how panic fits into our lives.

Mapping Spiritual Care and Therapy

The classical tradition of spiritual care centers on *soul curing* rather than *problem solving*. From a soul-making perspective, presenting problems are about life and its growing edges. In spiritual care a presenting problem is listened to as a life story. However, in the pastoral care literature, pastoral counseling is not confined to only one kind of approach but is located all over the map. Howard Clinebell's 1984 revised edition of *Basic Types of Pastoral Care and Counseling* generously includes all the essential therapies till the 1980s as potential pastoral care and counseling resources. Donald Capps's *Reframing: A New Method in Pastoral Care* (1995) and *Living Stories: Pastoral Counseling in the Congregational Context* (1997) completes the Therapeutic Strategies Map (Figure 4.1) by the addition of postmodern therapies as the latest methods in the ministry of pastoral care. Howard Stone (1994, 1999, 2000) has widely written on *Brief Pastoral Counseling* (1944; see also 1999, 2000), contesting the need to focus on the root causes of problems and the belief that long-term therapy has better durability of benefits than brief methods in pastoral counseling.

Charles Gerkin in *The Living Human Document: Re-Visioning Pastoral Counseling in a Hermeneutical Mode* (1989) criticizes the pastoral counseling alliances with the various secular psychological theories and schools of therapy. He emphasizes the pastoral integrity inherent in the conversational/narrative approach that privileges the language of faith and theology as autonomous voices in the process of interpreting the meanings we live by. The presenting problem in the "hermeneutical mode" is the "constructed," "languaged" problem. It is a subjectivist and intrinsic problem definition and the pastoral conversation is focused on the "text" of the "living human document." Gerkin argues for the inherent compatibility between a spiritual perspective and the hermeneutical mode that incorporates reflection and interpretation of our life experience.

An exploration of the different ways of defining and resolving problems reveals that spiritual care addresses a wide scope of problem situations and thus stands to benefit from a comprehensive array of strategies. In the history of pastoral care, the three common images of the pastor, *shepherd*, *wounded healer*, and *wise fool*, attest to the diversity in functions (see Campbell, 1981). The *shepherd* fits the "objectivist problem resolution" description, and can be expressed in active intervention (the care-taking function) or in authoritative counsel (the guiding function). The *wounded healer* fits the "subjectivist problem resolution" approach to problems that are extrinsically defined in terms of personal and relational dynamics. The *wise fool* also fits the "subjectivist problem resolution" approach but with an intrinsic focus on how the problem is constructed and scripted. The attempt to embrace multiple roles in spiritual care in figure 4.2, following the *Therapeutic Strategies Map*, is not so much to generate another classification model as to demonstrate that spiritual care and therapy cannot be confined to a narrow, purist perspective.

Figure 4.2   Multiple Roles Map

Objectivist Problem Resolution

Action Orientation
- "What to do"

Theory Orientation
- "What to know"

SHEPHERD - CARETAKER

SHEPHERD - GUIDE

Intrinsic

Extrinsic

Problem Definition

Problem Definition

Text Orientation
- "What to understand"

Person Orientation
- "What to be"

WISE FOOL

WOUNDED HEALER

Subjectivist Problem Resolution

Conclusion

The focus on problem definition and problem resolution has taken on special urgency. The politics of managed care requires problems to be defined in terms of their resolutions. To many caregivers, the problem-solving success orientation of managed care is clearly antithetical to the soul-curing life perspective of spiritual care. Yet, drawing the connections between problem definitions and problem resolutions is what constitutes a model of care. How the problem is defined in therapy determines how it is addressed, and how the problem is addressed defines the model of care. The two are reciprocally connected.

The days of fierce competition when schools of therapy recruited "true believers" seem to be past. Today the ideal is for professional caregivers to develop their own integrative model and style of caring. This chapter assumes that students in a clinical education program need to know not just one (supposedly the "best" one), but all the dozen or so essential psychotherapies if personal integration is to occur (Gurman & Messer, 1995, 1). As an inclusive study and diversified clinical practice clarify these therapy models are distinct in fundamental ways. They:

- Stem from different views of human nature
- Embrace various ways of getting to know clients
- Encompass distinct visions of reality (Gurman & Messer, 1995, 2).

This chapter has located spiritual care and counseling across the various schools of therapy, with special mention of the hermeneutical approach in its thrust toward meaning-making. Other chapters will continue with incorporating the therapies toward a broadly based integration of the theory and practice of spiritual care. The maps in this chapter cover four quadrants, each representing one perspective of a specific problem-definition/resolution fit. Such a map invites presenting problems to be navigated across the board, looking at them from different angles. This principle of perspectivism affirms multiple therapeutic roles and strategies, validating the essential therapies as potential resources in spiritual care and therapy.

CHAPTER 5

What to Say:
Therapeutic Communication

ANITA, AN INTERN in a family therapy program, presented in group supervision a videotape of a conflicted counseling session. As background she reported that she had seen Shirley in individual counseling for three sessions. During that time it had become increasingly apparent that Shirley attributed most of her problems to the "overbearing" behavior of her husband Jim. Anita had asked for a joint session in order to get Jim's perspective on the troubled relationship and to explore the possibility of couple counseling. The tape showed Anita warmly welcoming Jim to the session, expressing her appreciation for his willingness to share his "side of the story." In the first thirty minutes Anita focused on Jim, at times rebuffing Shirley's interruptions to "correct" or "explain" Jim's account. The critical incident that Anita had selected for supervision occurred when Shirley suddenly got up, ready to leave, shouting: "I might as well go and let the two of you decide what the hell is going on in the marriage."

Supervision could explore a variety of questions. One could be a "what to understand" question such as: Did the counseling session parallel Shirley's marital experience of getting shut up? Another could be a "what to be" question: Did Anita unwittingly align with Jim in a triangle against Shirley's critical voice and thus abandon her client? This chapter will present what could be called a "what to communicate" approach, focusing on the actual *words* of the therapeutic intervention. Anita presented for supervision her response to Shirley:

> Shirley, I really want you to stay, because I need the two of you here if we are to make sense of what is going on in the marriage. The reason why I have concentrated on getting connected with Jim, understanding his point of view, is because I need to balance the time I have had with you. We can only do couple work when Jim gets on board.

In consulting the *Therapeutic Strategies* (TS) *Map* from the previous chapter, Anita's response fits in the top left quadrant: it intrinsically defines the problem (Shirley's objection to Anita's concentrating on and privileging Jim), and proposes to resolve the problem objectively (based on the therapist's expert rationale of getting Jim on board). In a response from the other end of the TS Map, Anita could say: *Gee Shirley, I was not aware how upsetting this has been for you. You feel excluded at this point and I want you to feel part of this conversation again.* This second response fits in the bottom right quadrant of the TS Map: it defines the problem extrinsically (Shirley's feeling of being excluded) and proposes to resolve the problem subjectively (an empathic identification with Shirley's feelings and inviting her in).

Figure 5.1   Locating Counseling Responses

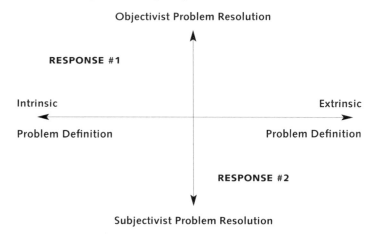

In a "what to say" approach, words are viewed as the navigators that maneuver the helping conversation on the map of therapeutic strategies. This focus on "what to say" appears to run counter to the spiritual care and pastoral counseling tradition where the dominant emphasis has been on "what to be" in the helping relationship. An exclusive "what to be" focus, however, can unduly simplify and restrict the dynamics of spiritual care. For spiritual caregivers, "what to be" has often been the simple yet profound experience of being simultaneously present and real in caring. Yet these assumptions of what is "present," and, even more unsettling, of what is "real," are at the very core of today's postmodern critique. In a world of multiple realities and multiple selves, "what to be" offers an infinite array of possible answers depending on such shifting dimensions as perspective, context and language. In this multi-textured world of possibilities and choices, the question of what to say has become more relevant in reflecting the many sides of spiritual care.

Three Styles of Therapeutic Communication

The curious fact of the "what to be" focus is that it tends to reduce the art of communication to the ability to listen. To quote from Paul Wachtel's definitive study of therapeutic communication: "Training programs continue to emphasize primarily the development of therapists' listening skills. They teach therapists (as, of course, they should) to cultivate an empathic capacity to enter into the patient's or client's world.... Implicitly or explicitly, the assumption is made that if one really understands, what to say will become clear rather readily" (1993, 1). This chapter will examine specific formulations of therapeutic communication in the context of different styles or genres of therapeutic conversation. In this context, "what to communicate" is different from "what to say" by going beyond words to a consideration of the matrix of meanings and process in which the conversation is embedded. In the following overview of styles of therapeutic communication, I will differentiate three roles of the caregiver: the *representative*, the *reflective* and the *reconstructive* role. These three styles construct the various strategies depicted on the Therapeutic Strategies Map and can be incorporated in the map as shown in Figure 5.2.

Figure 5.2   Locating Communication Styles

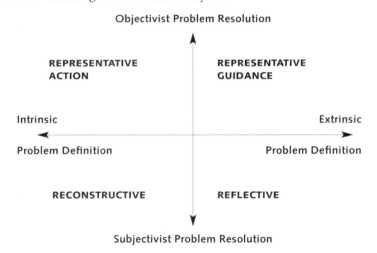

Objectivist Problem Resolution

REPRESENTATIVE
ACTION

REPRESENTATIVE
GUIDANCE

Intrinsic

Extrinsic

Problem Definition

Problem Definition

RECONSTRUCTIVE

REFLECTIVE

Subjectivist Problem Resolution

The Representative Role

The *representative* role in therapeutic communication focuses on the counselor as the messenger who knows and delivers a message from an authoritative source. In the classical pastoral tradition, the representative role is defined in terms of a faithful and informed adherence to and symbolic performance reflecting a sacred reality believed to be of ultimate significance. Other helping professionals are similarly educated and "anointed" by society as keepers of specialized knowledge and performers of specific rites of healing.[1]

There has been much justified apprehension about abuses stemming from a power differential inherent in specialized knowledge, skills and position. In our postmodern period there has been a concerted effort not to grant the professional person privileged status. The attribution of special professional expertise easily contaminates the helping relationship. Professional helpers can become overwhelmed by exorbitant demands of high client expectations, and clients can be exploited in boundary violations by presumptions of professional arrogance and entitlement.

Despite the potential of abuse, the representative role in the helping professions is an essential one. The position of a spiritual caregiver or pastor is similar to that of other trained helping professionals with special areas of expertise. People look to spiritual caregivers for various kinds of resources: from insight into the meaning of religious faith, to practical guidance in dealing with family difficulties or vocational choices, to spiritual support in sustaining the stresses of life. Despite well-grounded suspicions of the politics of special knowledge and truth claims, informed guidance, whether academic, clinical or professional, represents potent health resources. All people need such assistance from time to time in order to manage the tasks of life and experience healing in the midst of the conflicts and indignities of life.

From a subjective, psychological perspective, the psychoanalytic school of *self psychology* describes the universal childhood need for merger with a source of idealized strength and calmness in times of crisis and anxiety.[2] Even though parents may have responded well (and many have not) to these childhood needs, there is ongoing human dependence on such parental support and guidance throughout life. This *idealizing transference*, the need to experience merger with greatness, strength and calm, energizes the counseling relationship where for many the spiritual counselor represents the wisdom of the faith community with a long tradition of religious and spiritual care.

Some expressions of representative communication, such as sermonizing, lecturing and moralizing, have become stereotypical for cartoons depicting pastoral conversations. More comprehensive, and less burdened, examples of representative communication in spiritual care include spiritual direction, practical advice, shared prayer, crisis intervention, utilization of community resources, educational instruction, and life-skill coaching. What these types of communication have in common is a proactive stand and a directive intervention style.

---

1 For a vivid description of "The Anointment of Professionals," see Marilyn R. Peterson, *At Personal Risk* (New York: Norton, 1992), 11-33.
2 For a discussion of the three "self-object transferences" see Heinz Kohut, *How Does Analysis Cure?* (Chicago: University of Chicago Press, 1984), 192-210.

▨ The Reflective Role

The *reflective* role in communication is for most caregivers a far more comfortable style of conversation than the representative approach. The reflective style does not claim external verities but articulates the subjective realities active within the counseling relationship. It is in tune with humanistic/existential theories and values the person's ability to access inner resources of knowledge and guidance. Reflective communication celebrates the person's special worth through the respectful attention of "active listening." This therapeutic rite of acceptance follows the process of empathically identifying with the person's inner experience of self and "being in the world." The caregiver is a grace-filled mirror that through "reflective" or "interchangeable" responses traces and honors the person's feelings, beliefs, hopes and aspirations.[3]

Reflective communication, however, reflects *both* partners in conversation. With good cause and humor, reflective communication has been caricatured as a one-way process: a mindless mechanical process of mimicking the client. True reflective communication occurs in the encounter of at least two persons and two worlds. Listening is prefaced and punctuated by "I messages." The caregiver as I-messenger reflects his or her own inner thoughts, feelings and curiosity, often in "low-level inferences" (when I hear you say...I feel, think, wonder...). This reciprocity is reflected when the term "caregiver" is changed to "caresharer." The two-sided mirror metaphor is rich in religious meanings and the main source of inspiration for the "what to be" focus of attending presence.

The mirror image is also a basic concept in developmental psychology. Being born without a self-concept, young children need adults who delight in them to mirror them. Madonna with child images project a universal icon: a child being reflected in the knowing and admiring eyes of the parent, eyes which mirror to the child his or her special being and calling in life. Self psychology describes this perennial, basic human need for acceptance and confirmation in *mirror transference,* where childhood "mirroring" needs are revived and nurtured in the presence of a "reflective" caregiver.

▨ The Reconstructive Role

The *reconstructive* role in communication take place in the ever emerging, ever-changing constructions of meaning in human experience.[4] Human beings are

---

3 For a full discussion of the various facilitative and blocking responses from a reflective communication perspective see the classic research study of C.B. Truax & R.R. Carkhuff in *Toward Effective Counselling and Psychotherapy* (Chicago: Aldine, 1967).

4 An eloquent exposition of therapeutic communication from a radical postmodern perspective appears in Jay S. Efran, Michael D. Lukens and Robert Y. Lukens, *Language Structure and Change: Frameworks of Meaning in Psychotherapy* (New York: Norton, 1990). For a pastoral counseling perspective, see Donald Capps, *Reframing: A New Method in Pastoral Care* (Minneapolis: Fortress, 1990), and *Living Stories: Pastoral Counselling in Congregational Context* (Minneapolis: Fortress, 1998).

defined as meaning-making creatures; not passive recipients of general knowledge that reflects external, objective realities, but active agents in generating highly particularized meanings and maps by which to live their lives. This constructivist process, however, is not a solitary one of separate minds but recruits cooperation from other meaning systems. Meaning-making constructs exist on many levels (individual, family, social, cultural, religious), which jointly co-author evolving life scripts.

Reconstructive communication is joining others in the meaning-making process of understanding, based on the belief that there are many ways to view the world and live our lives. Rigid personal constructs often hamper a person's social integration or constrict his or her range of responses to new situations. Reconstructive communication seeks to clear these obstacles by enhancing a person's adaptive, creative abilities to live life. In such a counseling process, the role of *empathy* is primary, though somewhat different from the empathy of the *reflective* style: "In constructivist terms, empathizing entails the therapist's attempt to build a bridge into the lived experience of the client in order to indwell there, to "try on" the often idiosyncratic meanings the client attributes to events and to communicate an understanding of the predicament embodied in the client's understanding of the presenting problem" (Niemeyer, 1996, 386).

Other types of reconstructive communication techniques or process directives that I have learned to value include:

- inviting and entertaining stories, images and metaphors to explore meaning constructs.
- accentuating and punctuating narrative themes as well as exceptions to the dominant themes.
- expanding and constricting areas for attention.
- wondering, sometimes by philosophical and theological inquiry, in fostering curiosity, ambiguity and mystery.
- brainstorming, sometimes in playful exercises or role-plays (consulting with the devil or other authorities), in courting and experiencing unconventional or contrasting perspectives.
- reframing, relabeling, humor and paradox, as ways to change often negative, debilitating meanings by unexpected, at times, startling contextual shifts.

Reconstructive communication is a collaborative process. In the process of meaning-reconstruction, the counselor actively participates in communication where change can emerge through shared understandings. If there is the infusion of an empowering transference, and I think there is, it is the experience of being in the presence of someone sufficiently alike for mutual understandings. Self psychology calls this the *alter-ego* or *twinship transference*, which nurtures the human need to be in the presence of essential likeness, the experience of being human among humans.

The above survey of distinct communication styles illustrates that therapeutic conversations come in various shapes and forms. All three communication styles can be appropriate expressions of spiritual care depending on the specific context. In providing specialized information or conducting worship, the representative role stands out. Being with those who suffer, the reflective stance often makes for the most sensitive fit. When grieving a major loss, a reconstructive approach can facilitate the painful task of adapting to disorienting change and redefining one's place in the world. Table 5.1 below demonstrates that therapeutic communication relates to a wide diversity of variables, which for analytical purposes can be sorted into three pure styles of conversation. In practice these styles blend into countless composites of unique therapeutic encounters.

Table 5.1   Three Styles of Therapeutic Communication:
A Table of Comparison

	Representative	Reflective	Reconstructive
Paradigm	classical	humanistic	constructivist
Stance	authoritative	authentic	participatory
Relationship	symbolic	personal	collaborative
Transference	idealizing	mirroring	partnering
Focus	the message	the relationship	the discourse
Truth	objective / normative	subjective / relative	multiple / perspectival

A Therapeutic Conversation

The following case example of a pastoral conversation is based on Jesus's conversation with Nicodemus recorded in chapter 3 of the Gospel of John. John's account of the conversation is rather cryptic and abrupt in its transitions, compensated by innumerable sermons dedicated to filling in the voids. The conversation in verses 1-11 sets the stage for Jesus's discourse in the subsequent verses. I will reconstruct the conversation between Jesus and Nicodemus following the broad outline of a narrative sermon preached by Helmut Thielicke (1962, 59-71) in the days after World War II in Germany. This sermon, like the text, is a pastoral conversation. There is a parallel process between Nicodemus who came to Jesus by night and Thielicke's parishioners who lived in the dark days after the desolation of war. The sermon starts:

In the night voices and noises come to life which we do not hear by day. When we walk through a dark wood by night, we hear very different and often more terrifying things than when the sun is shining through the branches. Even within ourselves there are voices by night that are not heard by day...The guilt of past days and nights stands up and begins to speak to us. And our pillow becomes a stone on which we can find no rest. It was such a night as this that Nicodemus came to Jesus (59, 60).

The following conversation between Jesus and Nicodemus is an adaptation of Thielicke's sermon, with a process commentary in the right margin:

Nicodemus:	Rabbi, we know that you are a teacher who has come from God; for no one can do these signs that you do apart from the presence of God.	*assigning representative role*
Jesus:	You are a teacher yourself. But tonight, you come as a student.	*joining; confirming his own teaching role*
Nicodemus:	Perhaps you can tell me more about your teachings of life with God.	*inviting*
Jesus:	I tell you, I cannot tell you anything.	*paradox*
Nicodemus:	I beg you pard...(*stunned*)	
Jesus:	No one can see life without being born from above.	*teaching*
Nicodemus:	How can that be? (*laughing*) I am a grown man, well into my middle years, established in life. Being born from above?	*arguing / debating*
Jesus:	You make a good argument.	*joining and constricting*
Nicodemus:	Can one enter a second time into the mother's womb and be born?	*arguing*
Jesus:	Sounds crazy to me too.	*constraining*
Nicodemus:	How can this come about? (*more urgent*)	*grasping*
Jesus:	What is born of the flesh is flesh, and what is born of the Spirit is spirit.	*reframing*
Nicodemus:	Being born...One cannot bear oneself, one must *be* born.	*searching*
Jesus:	You say you cannot bring about your own birth. You are right. Born of the Spirit is like being blown by the wind. The wind blows where it chooses, you hear the sound of it, but do not know where it comes from or where it goes.	*empathizing* *teaching by metaphor*

Nicodemus:	But the wind is blowing…	*meaning-making*
Jesus:	And tomorrow the sun will be shining. You don't need to catch the sun into the net of your life.	*collaborating*
Nicodemus:	And I don't need to catch the wind…	*partnering*
Jesus:	You could leap into it.	*affirming / challenging*

This conversation maintains the original *representative* format of a teaching discourse as recorded in John's gospel. The initial exchanges set the stage for a courteous conversation structured along the complementary roles of teacher and student. The paradoxical response from Jesus—"I tell you, I cannot tell you"— marks a sudden and radical shift in the format of the conversation. What Nicodemus is asking for—"life with God"—is not a topic for polite conversation or stimulating debate of interesting ideas. Thielicke's sermon accentuates an existential gospel of commitment: "Jesus is known only in discipleship, or he is not known at all. All other talk about him is only religious shadow-boxing, which leads to no results and in which he refuses to take part…." While John's account of the conversation sounds harsh, likely part of a larger political polemic—"are you a teacher of Israel, and yet you do not understand these things?"—the above sermonic version is friendlier and therapeutic in tone. In the margin I note several instances where Jesus joins with Nicodemus and where he refrains from reactive, argumentative comebacks by constricting and restraining responses. Of special note is the *reflective* moment of empathic understanding when Jesus catches Nicodemus's sense of helplessness: "One cannot bear oneself, one must be born." Thielicke comments: "We can clearly hear Nicodemus's inner outburst: How can this be? Perhaps it is grace, but do you not see that grace here is of the utmost horror? Is it not terrible that the decisive point in my life should depend on something over which I have not the slightest influence?" The tension of Nicodemus's felt impasse polarizes the teacher-student split: one who knows in contrast to one who does not. The surprise in the concluding part of the conversation is a shift to a *reconstructive* style where the teacher-student split resolves sufficiently for a joint, almost playful, process of meaning-making to emerge.

An Application in Supervision

The above case example of a therapeutic conversation illustrates the many layers, the interplay of various styles of communication, in such encounters. There is no single formula for defining conversations as spiritual care. In contrast to the "what to be" focus, the "what to communicate" approach is multi-dimensional, combining empathic and contextual sensitivity with a flexible and strategic use of words and phrasing in therapeutic communication. Yet in supervision, the actual words easily get short thrift, minimized as technical details, with the real attention focused on understanding the larger relational picture or the psychodynamics of the counseling situation. The earlier case illustration of Anita's critical incident presented in supervision demonstrates how "mere" words constitute and construct the multiple realities in the counseling situation.

In supervision the *what to communicate* approach focuses on the actual words of the therapeutic intervention and utilizes the critical incident as a teachable moment in entertaining alternative ways to phrase helpful communication. Anita presented for supervision her response to Shirley:

> Shirley, I really want you to stay, because I need the two of you here if we are to make sense of what is going on in the marriage. The reason why I have concentrated on getting connected with Jim, understanding his point of view, is because I need to balance the time I have had with you. We can only do couple-work when Jim gets on board.

Although this statement reflected in clear "I-messages" her rationale for what she had done, Anita felt some discomfort about it. After having listened again to the tape, Anita shared her sense that it sounded somewhat defensive, perhaps even critical of Shirley: she should have known better. Her counseling response fits the *representative* communication style: informing Shirley that Anita had followed appropriate professional protocol in "balancing" the counseling relationship. Anita spoke from an authoritative position of in-house knowledge that guides responsible counseling practices. Yet in an emotionally charged context of blame, a "representative" role can easily distance the counselor in a perceived stance of professional aloofness and personal self-justification.

The benefit of group supervision is that it embodies a variety of perspectives and styles of practice. In exploring other options of "what to communicate," the following responses were role-played:

- I see that you are very upset and I realize now how hurtful it has been that I have not really given much attention to you—kind of ignored you. Especially after having had our one-to-one sessions, this might have felt like a sudden desertion....

- You are really angry—and I feel really bad that you have not felt part of the discussion. I wonder what it will take for you to want to stay rather than leave....

- It scares me that you feel bad enough to want to leave. It feels as if I have failed you. Perhaps you want to leave because you feel that I have left you and gone to Jim's side.

Generally, group members rated these responses as helpful. In all the three statements *reflective* characteristics dominate through expressions of personal caring and genuineness, empathic understanding, and lack of argumentative or defensive reactivity. The second response contains a *reconstructive* note by refocusing the wish to leave to a wish to stay. The third statement includes a *representative* line by suggesting a psychological interpretation of the client's wish to leave. Some in the supervision group questioned whether a volatile crisis situation is an appropriate context for reflective interactions: "therapy-talk" may fan rather than cool the heat of anger. I prefer the following suggested intervention:

> You are right! I have been so intent to get Jim here on board that I have neglected to pay attention to you. I have been so sure of my connection with you, and so anxious about having none with Jim, that I have taken our relationship for granted. What I really appreciate, Shirley, is your gutsiness to stand up and call me to task. That takes a lot of courage and honesty. I wonder whether this also happens in your relationship with Jim, or whether you are holding back a bit....

These words reframe Shirley's personal attack as courageous and helpful. The counselor not only accepts the validity of the accusation but also expands its meaning, including the paradoxical reframe that the counselor has been *too* "sure" of her connection with the client, sure enough to take it for granted. The *reflective* I-messages reaffirm that the counselor is "on her side." The *reconstructive* impact of the words is in the construction of a new therapeutic reality, no longer bound by the adversarial dynamics set up by the angry outburst. Having returned to a therapeutic world, the counselor does not miss a beat as she connects, in parallel fashion, the counseling process between client and counselor with the marital process between wife and husband.

Conclusion

The above case study in supervision highlights the linguistic structure of therapeutic conversations. The "what to communicate" dimension differentiates the various faces of the caregiver's presence: representative, reflective and reconstructive. The case study, also makes clear that the once prominent role of representing specialized or sacred knowledge has declined in our present information culture. The opposite is the case with the significance of the reflective role that has been universally acknowledged as the cornerstone of all effective communication. The reflective role has been further stretched to accommodate the diverse realities and contexts in the postmodern world. The reconstructive role in communication, which not only reflects but actively participates in constructing places of meaning and healing, is especially relevant for spiritual care and counseling, where people struggle to reframe the incomprehensible and destructive events of their lives within the perspective of a caring and intelligent universe.

CHAPTER 6

◈ What to Be:
Therapeutic Relationships

MARK CAME FOR THERAPY as a depressed teacher who dreads the prospect of returning to the classroom now that his sick leave is ending. His pain and confusion are clear:

> I really don't know what to do...whether to go back to teaching school. Ah—I can hardly stand the damn thought...but, you know, a stable job—a decent salary.... Or else make a clean break, likely go back to university and find something I can get excited about....

Such despondent words from a person reaching out for help often trigger an instinctive, instantaneous, and automatic inclination in the therapist to respond in a certain manner. These *countertransferences*, experiences that are evoked in the encounter and projected onto the client stem from the therapist's own life, often the family of origin (Stalfa, 1994). In understanding our countertransferences we become aware of the needs that we as caregivers bring to the helping relationship. The more aware we are of our needs as a helper, the less we demand of our clients and the less insistent we are concerning what helping style to employ. James Hillman speaks of countertransferences, the personal needs that we as therapists bring, as archetypal helping images:

The other person in a therapeutic encounter can serve any of these needs. His [sic] therapy therefore begins with my therapy, my becoming conscious of the various archetypal images which play through me and force the other into a role he may not be meant to play. For if I am a father, he must become a child; if I am a healer, he must be ill; and if I am enlightened, he must be benighted and astray. These images are part of the set, the scenic background into which, as on to a stage, the other makes his entry...The less I am aware of my personal needs and how they filter the forces playing through me, the more the archetypal aspects appear directly and impersonally. Counseling is then suddenly plunged into subhuman depths and the demands become inhuman from both parties. (1967, 19-20)

Spiritual care does not require that we strip ourselves of countertransferences and divest ourselves of the need to help. It does mean that as helpers we must be sufficiently aware of our needs to help to begin to move beyond a dominant helping style. This chapter explores how styles of care can be monitored and transformed through the differentiation process.

Two dominant countertransferences are distinguished: the inner pull to be with the person in need and share the person's pain, and the inner push to rescue the person from the pain. The one response stands out in the *empathizer*, the other in the *rescuer*. The two countertransferences exemplify two helping modalities: the *being with* mode of the facilitative use of self, and the *doing for* mode of the directive use of self. These modalities reflect two prominent but contrary models of spiritual care, set apart by radically different styles of care: *compassion* and *competence*.

The Compassion Model

The compassionate caregiver is deeply touched by a person's pain and moved to share and alleviate the suffering. Through compassion the caregiver participates in and identifies with the suffering. Attachment theory describes a similar dynamic in parent-child interactions where helpers draw close to those who signal distress as they feel abandoned, threatened, and insecure.

Compassion carries deeply spiritual connotations related to human vulnerability and our transitory place in the world. Such is the case in existential therapist Irvin Yalom's "tale of psychotherapy," *I never thought it would happen to me*. In the story an older woman is grieving the loss of her husband, followed less than two years later by a brutal purse snatching. Left with post-traumatic stress symptoms of overwhelming feelings of isolation and preoccupation with her safety, she entered therapy. The robbery went beyond her purse and touched her place in the world: "That sense of specialness, of being charmed, of being the exception, of being eternally protected-all those self-deceptions that had served her so well suddenly lost their persuasiveness. She saw through her own illusions, and what illusion had shielded now lay before her, bare and terrible. Her grief wound was now fully exposed" (Yalom, 1989, 149).

The compassion model rests on a powerful base: the wounded person's experience of pain generates the gravitational pull that draws the helper through empathic identification. This baseline in the wounded person is represented by a line of interaction between *suffering* and *knowing* the wound. Knowing is found in the ongoing process of naming, interpreting, and representing the wound through such narrative and symbolic expressions as story, lamentation, prayer, and symptom. The knowing and suffering interaction keeps the wound, though rooted in the past, hurting in the present and projected through anticipation into the future.

The caregiver connects with the suffering primarily through what the wounded person knows and tells about the wound. The bridge of empathic involvement is the connecting link with the suffering person. Knowing and suffering are reciprocally related: the knowledge of the wound informs and shapes the suffering as much as the suffering informs and shapes the knowledge. Compassion lies in knowing and feeling the wound. In compassion, knowing is loving, with an intensity that unites. Yalom expresses empathic identifications with the grieving widow when he says: "It's so hard for me, too, to accept that all these afflictions—aging, loss, death—are going to happen to me too" (1989, 150).

Figure 6.1   The Compassion Model

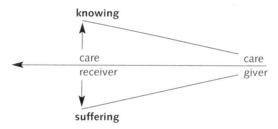

The compassion model embodies a profoundly spiritual approach in caregiving. Being present offers a place of empathic solidarity and understanding. This presence goes beyond empathy in pointing to a spiritual presence, or to a God who remembers us. This is prominent in the Christian tradition where the ministry of presence is *incarnational* presence, modeled after the image of the Christ who identified himself with human suffering unto death. The incarnation encompasses the full range of human experience but culminates in ultimate suffering. The crucifixion surrounds us with the stark images of trauma: the bloody torture to death, the rejection, and loneliness of the cross, the abandonment by God.

The traumatic dimensions in suffering dramatize both the intrinsic genius and the hazards of the compassion model. Trauma represents intense suffering that increasingly cripples and disrupts the person's perspective and functioning in life. Trauma is the wound that multiplies through persisting, intrusive thoughts, dreams, images, and flashbacks. As wounding approximates trauma, the suffering person will lose the ability to name the pain, paralyzed by what cannot be grasped or expressed. Trauma is the pain that breaks the connection between knowing and feeling the suffering. Greg Mogenson, in a book aptly titled *God is a Trauma*, describes how trauma in its overwhelming claims on the psyche functions as a god: "Just as God has been described as transcendent and unknowable, a trauma is an event which transcends our capacity to experience it. Compared to the finite nature of the traumatized soul, the traumatic event seems infinite, all-powerful, and wholly other" (1989, 1-2). Trauma in this demanding, god-like impact creates and organizes life after its own image.

As presented in the triangular diagram in Figure 6.1, the more traumatically charged the suffering, the more compassion will be generated and the closer the caregiver will be drawn into the cycle of trauma incapacitation. The identification with overwhelming suffering in the wounded person will heighten the empathy countertransference, sensitizing and activating the caregiver's own woundedness. This reciprocal process will increasingly put the caregiver at risk of the debilitating impact of what has been aptly labeled "compassion fatigue" or "vicarious traumatization."

The Competence Model

In the compassion model empathy propels the caregiver into the inner dynamics of knowing and suffering in the wounded person. In the competence model the lure of the counselor's expertise propels the careseeker to outer resources offered through the caregiver. Thus the two models share similar triangular diagrams that are mirror images of one another.

Figure 6.2   The Competence Model

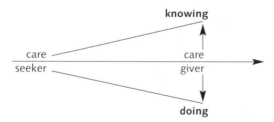

The competence model provides a point of connection outside the troubled, and in traumatized lives flooded, inner world of not knowing and the resulting hopelessness of mindless suffering. The caregiver offers outer perspectives and resources to facilitate the wounded person's going beyond the confines of private suffering. As a trained professional, the caregiver draws from her or his helping image, spiritual and religious tradition, clinical wisdom and expertise to provide new and authoritative perspectives of knowing and doing in addressing the woundedness. Yalom goes beyond empathy; informed by his existentialist perspective, he tells his grieving patient: "You must feel that if Albert were alive, this would never have happened to you. So the robbery brings home the fact that he's really gone. You knew that before, I know. But part of you didn't. Now you really know that he's dead. He's not in the yard. He's not out back in the workshop. He's not anywhere. Except in your memories" (1989, 150).

The wounded client's knowing is not just mirrored but expanded, confronted or edited by the caregiver. In clinical psychology the knowing and doing of the caregiver lie in the link between diagnosis and treatment. Diagnosis presents the so-called "objective" knowledge of suffering, the knowledge that maintains clinical distance by reflecting extensive case study research with generalized profiles of the symptoms of distress. Treatment becomes evidence-based therapy as it is guided by the link that ties diagnostic criteria to the clinical research of preferred outcomes and interventions.

It is interesting to note the similarities between the classical method of pastoral care and the modern clinical model. Classical pastoral care and counseling emphasizes an objective message from sacred scripture and traditions of care while minimizing the more subjective process of empathic understanding in the pastoral relationship. The ministry of preaching eclipses the ministry of listening. Chrysostom, generally considered the greatest Christian preacher of antiquity, provides an example of a pastor who never really leaves the pulpit. In a "letter to a young widow," he excuses himself for not writing to her earlier since she could not have heard him in the time of her acute grief, "but when the troubled water has begun to subside, and the fury of the waves is abated, one can spread the sails of conversation" (Volz, 1990, 157). Classical grief counseling stressed moderation and control of one's grief, to highlight the comfort of the gospel, and fearing that our own private suffering may compete with the sufferings of Christ. Placing our sufferings in a faith context connects our personal story to the larger story of the faith community.

The value of the competence model is that it provides an external reference point for a closed system of suffering and a boundary for the caregiver who is at risk of being drawn into and traumatized by the cycle of woundedness. The model's hazards, however, signal caution to most therapists. The caregiver role in the competence model is primarily one of the expert whose task is to manage the wounded person's pain or save his or her soul. The model's focus is on the competence of a caregiver in complementary relationship with the helplessness of a care-receiver. Its toxic potential is great: a rigid rescuer-victim scenario organized by power differences that collapse only when therapy fails, often with helper and client feeling victimized by one another.

The Differentiation Model

The two models alone, shaped by compassion and competence, are often experienced and presented as diametrically opposed and mutually exclusive styles of therapy. From this polarized perspective, the therapist in the compassion model does not know and needs to listen to the client, while the competence model, the client does not know and needs to listen to the therapist.

In clinical education programs, supervisors often experience this difference in students. One student enters a practicum program primarily because of feelings of professional inadequacy, searching for good theory and techniques that work. In supervision this student asks, with an urgency directly proportionate to the degree of difficulty in the case presented, what to know and what to do. Another student appears far more confident, to the point of arrogance, secure in the ability of developing close relationships with clients and claiming inside knowledge of what is going on with the client. While the one student looks primarily for the clinical expert, if not the miracle worker, in the supervisor, the other student is more interested in a supervisory relationship that can support and parallel the relational dynamics of the counseling experience presented for supervision.

Table 6.1   Two Models of Care: Compassion and Competence:
A Table of Differentiation

Perspectives	Compassion Model	Competence Model
pastoral paradigm	relational pastoral	classical pastoral
"wounded healer" image	the woundedness in the healer	the healer in the woundedness
therapy mode	"being with"	"doing for"
power distribution	horizontal	vertical
therapist role	companion	coach
gravitation pull	into the suffering	into the helping
therapy direction	towards client	towards counselor
therapy resources	inner	outer
counseling style	facilitative	directive
use of self	personal empathy	clinical expertise
countertransference	the "empathizer"	the "rescuer"

From a self-differentiation perspective, the compassion and competence models are not opposites but the offspring of the same parent of anxiety. Empathy, anxious to connect with the person in pain, readily dissolves into emotional fusion, and seriousness, anxious to offer competent help, easily gets stuck in rescuing attempts. Such seriousness is contrasted with a therapeutic culture of playfulness that differentiates. This playfulness "has less to do with 'one-liners' than with the concept of flexible distance; it has less to do with good 'come-backs' than with the ability to distinguish process from content"

(Friedman, 1985, 51). Self-differentiated caring is a paradoxical concept that easily jars spiritual care sensitivities. Terms like *creative indifference, holy detachment*, and *benign neglect* point to the paradox of distancing as a playful form of therapeutic care. Such playfulness, rather than callous disregard, pays serious respect to the troubled and wounded as capable and creative people.

The differentiation model does not present a separate, third model of spiritual care. Rather it stresses an approach where the therapist can have recourse to both styles of care, without being identified with either one of them. It proposes a working alliance between the two students mentioned above: an alliance based on the ability to differentiate between compassion and competence. By helping archetype, temperament, and clinical experience, caregivers can move along a continuum from the compassion model to the competence model. A caregiver is not restricted to a fixed point on the continuum but can self-differentiate and balance the two ends on the continuum according to what is appropriate in a particular helping situation.

Such differentiation is expressed both in what the therapist *knows* and the counselor *does*. The integrated model of differentiation separates the two types of knowledge—the inner, subjective source of the pain and the outer reflection in therapy—and in so doing separates the wounded from the wound. This differentiation creates space for therapeutic conversations and critical reflection. In the psychoanalytic tradition this is where "soul-making" takes place. In his discussion of the omnipotent demands of trauma, Mogenson quotes James Hillman on the meaning of "soul" and on the need for differentiation for the soul to do its work:

> By *soul* I mean…a perspective rather than a substance, a viewpoint toward things rather than a thing itself. This perspective is reflective; it mediates events and makes differences between ourselves and everything that happens. Between us and events, between the doer and the deed, there is a reflective moment—and soul-making means differentiating this middle ground. (Mogenson,1989, 6)

The differentiation principle informs constructivist and hermeneutic theories when they prescribe a "not-knowing" stance for therapists. In order to learn from the client, the therapist becomes the curious listener who does not yet know but eagerly wants to know. True understanding is not separate from the listening process and imported into the counseling session. The therapist's pre-understandings are not only irrelevant but will obstruct the helping process and thus need to be checked at the door.

This "not knowing" emphasis, however, cannot be simply identified with the empathic presence of the compassion model. The therapeutic not-knowing stance does not mean that the therapist is totally dependent on the client for knowing anything at all. Rather, the counselor's not-knowing teases out unique bits of new and relevant knowledge and dares therapeutic competence to evolve in the helping dialogue itself. Healing happens in encounters that mutually enlighten client and therapist, opening windows of understanding and hope, going beyond the restrictive and oppressive walls of blind suffering. The Rogerian term *active listening* described the therapist's focus on understanding the client's inner world of feelings and thoughts. The term *active learning* may better fit a collaborative process where the therapist is responding both to the wounded person and to himself or herself in meaning-making conversation. Active learning is being poised for surprises, ready to pick up on what is novel and redemptive, what White and Epston have referred to as "unique outcomes" and "news of difference" (1985, 49) in stories otherwise saturated with doom and dominated by failure. In active learning, the listening ear is teamed with the playfulness of the reporter who can punctuate, organize, format the materials and suggest a headline, possibly a cartoon, to go with the story.

Differentiation in knowing is paralleled with a differentiation in doing. Rabbi Edwin Friedman applies the biological systems concept of self-differentiation to spiritual care. In an "emotional system" organized by pain the counselor is easily drawn into a triangle consisting of the client, his or her woundedness or problem, and the counseling role to support (the compassion model) or to rescue (the competence model) the person. Rather than a pastoral stance of uniting with the client in support and comfort, Friedman proposes the more controversial approach of *challenging*: "it requires one to non-anxiously tolerate pain, and even to stimulate pain, thus forcing the other to increase his or her threshold" (1985, 49). Friedman presents *challenge* as a radical shift in therapy, appealing to practices in modern healing of injecting germs and viruses directly into an organism so as to stimulate its own immune system.

Yalom's ability to differentiate compassion and competence is equaled by balancing seriousness with playfulness with his grieving and traumatized patient. When she is sobbing in the pain of ultimate isolation he points to her purse—"that same ripped-off, much-abused purse"—and says: "'Bad luck is one thing, but aren't you asking for it carrying around something that large?'" Taking the bait she hoists her purse on the table, emptying its content to prove that she needs everything in it. They banter about everything: the roll of fifty dimes, three bags of candy, a plastic bag of old orange peels, three pairs of sunglasses, a small stapler. "In that one hour, Elva moved from a position of forsakenness to one of trust. She came alive and was persuaded, once more, of her capacity for intimacy" (1989, 151).

Summary

The differentiation model joins rather than rejects the two triangles that represent the compassion and the competence models. The two triangles in interaction become a diamond that can contract and expand as it balances each triangle in shifting therapeutic alliances between the two ways of knowing and doing. This chapter, with its focus on *what to be* in spiritual care and therapy, highlights the therapeutic relationship as the place for negotiating the therapist's expertise in knowing and doing. Therapy as a science and craft is transformed into an art through the differentiation model. In therapy, differentiation becomes evident in the interplay between *what to know* and *what to do* in a therapist's flexible and playful ways of *what to be*. In the differentiation model, spiritual care is about the curious paradox that by learning from the other, the other can know, and that by defining oneself, others can find themselves.

CHAPTER 7

◈ The Helping Style Inventory: A Synthesis

THE PRECEDING THREE CHAPTERS charted the clinical triad of essentials in the practice of care: theory, practice, and the therapeutic relationship. In these demarcations I am guided by the history of the Clinical Pastoral Education (CPE) movement, which can be roughly organized into three main sections that highlight its theology and practice of ministry (Powell, 1975). The first stage centered on *what to do* and emphasized communication skills and active ability in helping people in distress. The goal was to see theology as an applied science and focus on practical interventions and social action. A next phase in the history of CPE emphasized *what to know*, holding that the special gift of pastoral care is not techniques but the insights and understandings it could bring to human suffering. Late in the 1950s the focus changed to *what to be*, emphasizing the helping relationship as the key to healing. In this view, pastoral care came of age when it disavowed both expert knowledge and clinical expertise as the primary tools in care. From this perspective, self-knowledge rather than theoretical knowledge and the use of the helping relationship rather than of techniques become the hallmarks of spiritual care.

This section combines knowing (*what to know*), doing (*what to say*) and being (*what to be*) in an interaction of three helping dynamics that are not to be ranked in a hierarchical order or put in competition. Rather, the three constitute an animated composite of variables that in conjunction shape the therapy. If there is any primacy, it is the helping relationship as it coordinates and attunes theory and practice to a particular therapy situation. This relational context signals a change from content to process and from the person as a solitary entity to the person in relationship. In this chapter on helping styles, spiritual care is described as the art of integrating *what to know* and *what to say* through the multiple ways of *what to be* in the therapeutic relationship. The chapter expands the differentiation model of the preceding chapter by focusing on the therapeutic relationship and including a variety of therapeutic modes predicated by the context of the encounter. As such the chapter is the synthesis and application of Part 2.

Mapping Therapy

Mark, the 38-year-old elementary school teacher in the previous chapter, is on sick leave because of "mental exhaustion." For six weeks he has been in therapy for his depression. Facing the approaching end of his leave of absence, he comes for his weekly therapy session drawn and tense, saying:

> I really don't know what to do … whether to go back to teaching school. Ah—I can hardly stand the damn thought … but, you know, a stable job—a decent salary…Or else make a clean break, likely go back to university and find something I can get excited about….

At this point the therapist also faces the question of "what to do." Hearing this cry of despondency and confusion, most therapists will feel some confusion over what to say as well as some question about the appropriateness of their first impulse concerning what to say. The sample helping responses below are to be rated neither as wrong or right, nor according to personal preference. Rather, these specific responses demonstrate a variety of therapeutic strategies:

1. I have the sense that this is a critical time in your life. You are at the midpoint of life, and may think you hear the last call. I think that it will be helpful to continue with therapy to get a better sense of who you are and where you best fit.

2. When I listen to you I hear two persons arguing about what decision Mark has to make. My concern is that you get caught between these two adversarial voices. Perhaps we can stop the fight and begin to listen to what each has to say—when they have a decent dialogue.

3. That's a really tough decision. It sounds like you are under a lot of stress right now. I admire your courage to acknowledge how frightening it is just thinking to go back to the classroom … the place that nearly did you in.

4. I think that all this inward fighting, trying to be being brave, is a way to not accept your depression. You know Mark, you have good reason to be depressed and perhaps you need to allow yourself to feel the depth of it.

These four responses illustrate examples of the *models of caring* on the Therapeutic Strategies (TS) Map (see chapter 4) in the four quadrants, each bounded by the horizontal continuum of an intrinsic *versus* an extrinsic problem definition, and by the vertical continuum of an objectivist *versus* a subjectivist approach in problem resolution. According to this map, the respective responses fit the following TS categories:

Response #1: An extrinsic problem definition (the problem is that Mark has a mid-years crisis) and an objectivist problem solution (based on therapy resources).

Response #2: An intrinsic problem definition (the problem is as reported, being caught between opposites) and a subjectivist problem solution is (the inner argumentation needs to be resolved into a dialogue).

Response #3: An extrinsic problem-definition (the problem is that the person is immobilized by fear) and the problem-resolution is subjectivistic (the person needs to feel understood and affirmed as courageous).

Response #4: An intrinsic problem definition (the problem is as reported, feeling depressed and helpless) and an objectivist problem resolution (the expertise of the therapist in relabeling the problem and offering a paradoxical remedy).

Figure 7.1   Locating "What to Do" Responses

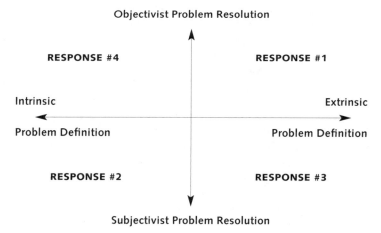

From the Therapeutic Strategies Map to the Helping Style Inventory

In chapter 5 the TS Map was viewed from the perspective of the words of caring. Words were depicted as the navigators that move helping responses across the board of potential therapeutic strategies. This chapter revisits the TS map from the perspective of helping styles. While the communication chapter was centered in the use of words, this chapter focuses on the use of self.

The *Helping Style Inventory* (HSI) (VanKatwyk, 1988, 1995) map follows the TS Map in utilizing a double-axis model of two dimensions that define helping interactions. The horizontal axis, in the TS Map describing how the problem is defined, becomes the *focus of attention* dimension on the HSI Map. This continuum stretches from one extreme, the task-orientation's focus on the presenting problem, to the other, the person-orientation's focus on the person's life as the problem situation affects and defines it.

Figure 7.2   The Horizontal HSI Axis

This horizontal scale draws a continuum from the perspective of the helper's "use of self." At the task-orientation end, the helper identifies primarily with the presenting problem and the client's perception of it. At the opposite end of the continuum, the helper identifies primarily with the client as encountered and understood in the problem situation.

This *focus-of-attention* dimension is subject to polarization into potentially opposing and mutually excluding positions. In the 1950s the prominent sociologist Talcott Parsons distinguished helping functions in the nuclear family through gender-specific roles: the breadwinner husband/father provided the family resources, while the homemaker wife/mother maintained supportive and integrative relations among family members (Parsons & Bates, 1955). While the traditional nuclear family has been largely replaced by more complex and fluid family structures, helping roles are still influenced by the ways of the past: men are seen as engaging in task-oriented relating, women in helping, person-oriented ones. Taking a sociolinguistic approach, Deborah Tannen argues that women and men come from essentially different cultures apparent in gender differences in conversational and helping styles. While men tend to concentrate on problem solving, women tend to focus on understanding the person with the problem (1990, 51, 52).

Spiritual care approaches to helping have traditionally emphasized that, rather than caring about the problem, care focuses on the soul: *cura animarum*. In common with existential and analytical psychotherapies, spiritual care and counseling has often been person oriented in its problem focus: rather than fixing problems or removing symptoms, the troubles of life are engaged and utilized as opportunities to examine one's life or save one's soul. Pastoral counselor John Patton raises the uniquely spiritual care question, "How can a person's problem be a context of care rather than the focus of care?" (1993, 56-57). At the same time it needs to be stressed again that spiritual care is not limited to a person orientation. Spiritual care and pastoral counseling are about life, and consequently address a broad scope of problems spanning both ends of the continuum.

The vertical axis is the *use of power* dimension in the helping relationship on the HSI map with a continuum stretching from the *directive* to the *facilitative* use of self.

Figure 7.3   The Vertical HSI Axis

The two ends of the continuum reveal two distinct styles in the use of power. The HSI uses the traditional psychotherapy terms directive and facilitative to distinguish between the two. The continuum goes from one extreme where the power to help is totally located in the helper, to the other extreme, where the power to help is totally located in the person seeking help. A *directive* use of power emphasizes the strengths of the professional helper—expert knowledge, clinical experience and/or charismatic or symbolic roles through which the helper represents a reality larger than his or her own personal presence. The disconcerting aspect of this helping scenario is that its script implies the complementarity of the "strong" helping the "weak." Public consciousness of the "weak" centers on those vulnerable to abuse: children, women, and the elderly. The awareness that all who receive care are at personal risk contributes to a "hermeneutics of suspicion" that sees the potential in directive use of power for the abuse of power.

In contrast, the *facilitative* use of power emphasizes the strengths of the persons seeking help in terms of their own personal agency and inner wisdom as well as resources available through their life experience and social supports. The disconcerting aspect of this scenario is the possibility that the helper needs to restrain the exercise of her or his own power to help so as not to interfere with the other person's strengths. Contrary to Rogerian ideals about the equal reciprocity of the therapeutic relationship, current professional codes of ethics rightly see helping relationships as unequal because of the inherent power differential. Paradoxically, the potential for abuse of power often fits more the facilitative than the directive approach. It is in the facilitative context, that not only is the power of the helper not openly acknowledged, at times it is even concealed by believing, or pretending, that it is not in use.

From this perspective, the two ends of the power continuum do not represent the relative presence or absence of the helper's use of power. The issue is not whether or not but *how* this power is being exercised: overtly or covertly, explicitly or implicitly. In the history of helping relationships these two styles in the use of power have often been experienced as contrary in value orientation and mutually exclusive in clinical practice. A common goal in most clinical education programs in spiritual care has been to move students from doing for to being with the person to be helped.

The HSI is constructed along two main dimensions that define the context of helping interactions. Both dimensions are visualized going from one extreme to another. It is understood that these two extreme ends reflect not so much real as hypothetical helping situations discussed for didactic purposes in visualizing the *focus of attention* and the *use of power* continuums.

Putting It All Together: The HSI Map

The HSI Map as a double-axis model produces four quadrants, which identify four helping styles and four helping images (going clockwise from the top):

Table 7.1   Four Styles and Four Images

Helping Style		Helping Image
1. Directively person-oriented	(dp)	*The Guide*
2. Facilitatively person-oriented	(fp)	*The Celebrant*
3. Facilitatively task-oriented	(ft)	*The Consultant*
4. Directively task-oriented	(dt)	*The Manager*

The four types of helping styles emphasize that multiple perspectives inform care and that the competent caregiver is characterized by a differential use of self. The HSI proposes an integrative approach to spiritual care and counseling. For the map to be useful as a teaching and supervision tool, specific helping behaviors are incorporated to define the practice of each helping style. This identification of specific behaviors does not pretend to provide a comprehensive classification. Rather it illustrates the distinctive behavioral features of each of the four helping styles.

Each of the helping behaviors is placed on a scale of three levels of intensity. For instance, the *guide* behaviors range from *informing* to *coaching* to *directing*. The less intense helping behaviors appear at the core while the next two levels of increasing intensity move toward the outside. The core area is closer and less shaded, signifying that core-area helping behaviors are less separated and differentiated (informing-connecting-conversing-suggesting), allowing the helper to shift easily from one style to another. The movement from the core to the outer rim, toward more shaded areas, leads to more pronounced and separated helping style behaviors. As such behaviors become more extreme, they increasingly confine the helper to one inflexible helping style to the exclusion of other options.

Figure 7.4 The Helping Style Inventory

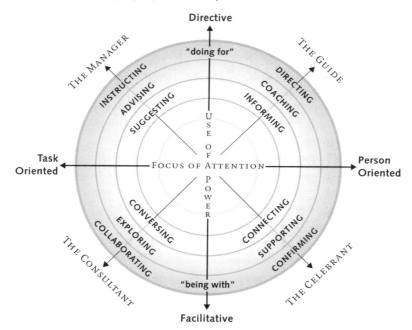

The HSI Map assumes that basic students in clinical education do best by concentrating on core-level helping behaviors. Students who enter clinical education programs with pronounced helping styles, such as found in directing/guiding or confirming/celebrating, tend to be more stuck in their specialized helping posture and less likely to expand their helper identity and skill repertoire as a caregiver. Advanced students, more mature in contextual sensitivity and skill competence, can profitably use the midrange, and at times even venture into more extreme helping responses as situationally appropriate, without necessarily locking themselves into a limited and rigid role in counseling.

HSI Verbatim Example

In the following counseling verbatim excerpt we return to Mark who is on sick leave from his teaching job (M = Mark; C = Counselor):

M1:   I really don't know what to do...whether to go back to teaching school. Ah—I can hardly stand the damn thought...but, you know, a stable job—a decent salary...Or else make a clean break, likely go back to university—find something I can get excited about....

C1:   The closer it gets for you to return to work, the bigger this inner turmoil...

M2:   I don't know...(*buries his head in his hands*)

C2:   You say, "I don't know," but I wonder whether you really *do* know what you want to do.

M3:   Perhaps I am too scared to really say...(*looking up*) that I don't want to go back to teaching.

C3:   Pretend that you are not scared. Tell people—your dad...your wife.... Right now tell me: "I don't want to go back to school."

M4:   I...I...don't want to go back...to school. (*haltingly*)

C4:   What is happening Mark?

M5:   God—my heart is pounding...(*begins to cry*) I can't even say it.

C5:   Perhaps you are not just disgusted with your job.... Perhaps you are also disgusted with yourself.

M6:   What do you mean?

C6:   I think I hear you berating yourself for not having the guts to quit.

M7:   Well, should I quit?

C7:   How important is it for you to know what others think what is best for you, and how concerned are you not to disappoint them?

M8:   I don't want to upset anyone. But it wouldn't be the first time that I disappoint my family....

C8:   I think, Mark, that the scariest thing in life is to leave, or to disappoint. Sometimes it is leaving home, or leaving a job..., or disagreeing with those who are close.

When the counselor's responses are inserted on the HSI Map, a counseling profile appears as presented in figure 7.5: the HSI Counseling Score. The diagram illustrates that the process of counseling is not confined to any one area on the HSI Map. In fact, the assumption of the HSI is that, ideally, the counselor moves about in a flexible use of a variety of styles.

The HSI encourages therapists to become more differentiated, creative, and flexible in their use of themselves, beyond the limiting choices of ideological preference and personal comfort.

Figure 7.5   The HSI Counseling Score

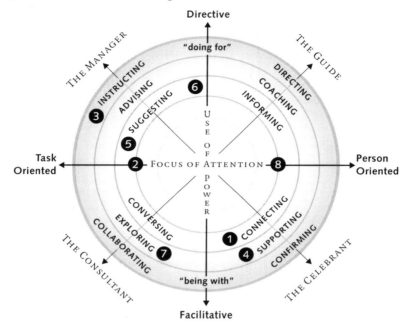

Applications for Clinical Education

Part 4, "The Study of Spiritual Care," profiles the HSI as the model for clinical education (see chapter 12). The HSI tool facilitates ways to learn a variety of helping skills through a flexible use of self. Students can approach counseling with the intimidating idea that there is one "right" way of therapy, hence feeling limited in experimenting with different helping interventions. The HSI encourages the exploration of new therapeutic territory with enhanced professional self-awareness. A larger repertoire of helping styles will provide the student with contextually appropriate choices beyond the restraints of personal or theoretical limitations.

Research studies of the implementation of the HSI in clinical education programs[1] seem to confirm that the HSI can be readily incorporated as a con-

---

1   In the unpublished HSI research study that won the 1987 Annual Research Award from the Canadian Association for Pastoral Practice and Education, Carrie Doehring tracked student learning curves through HSI coded verbatims. Thomas O'Connor et al., in the article "Diversity in the Pastoral Relationship: An Evaluation of the Helping Styles Inventory," (*The Journal of Pastoral Care* [49: 4, 1995], 365-374) present an ethnographic study of practitioners' experiences of the HSI, analyzing the data from twenty-one interviews, noting helpful and limiting aspects of the HSI, concluding that the "HSI is an effective tool in celebrating diversity" in the therapeutic relationship.

ceptual model that becomes available as a self-monitoring tool in counseling and supervision. Counseling scenarios, whether in written form or performed in role-play, provide a choice of intervention options. These choices configure the student's preferred helping style and mark the growing edges in her or his personal and professional use of self in therapy.

Correlating counseling scenario questionnaires with taped counseling sessions measures the level of congruence between the student's espoused theory of spiritual care and the actual practice of counseling. My experience has been that the majority of students in theory reject the manager helping image, yet many of them do employ manager helping behaviors (suggesting, advising) in their counseling practices. Conversely, students who view human nature as defective and in need of corrective guidance often adopt a non-directive and predominantly facilitative helping stance in therapy. The interaction between theory and practice, views of reality and helping interventions, is at the core of the HSI. Helping styles are grounded in actual therapy interactions yet inspired by models of care. The various ways in which the HSI model can be applied as a conceptual tool (in self-monitoring, teaching, and supervising) and as a catalyst (in critical reflection on the beliefs and practices of care) illustrate its inclusive and contextual approach to therapy.

PART THREE

Contexts
of
Caring

CHAPTER 8

◈ Toward a Balanced Whole: The Family Connection

IN THE WORLD OF THERAPY, the family plays a dominant and crucial role. The family is a person's earliest and most enduring connection to the world. Therapists have been prone to locate the cause of their clients' presenting problems or misery in the family connection; whether the more distant birth family or the immediate family by affiliation. Psychological assessments often focus on what was traumatic in the client's early family experience, something so enduring that it gets re-enacted in the present. Psychoanalytic theory eloquently describes how, in the first few years of life, family relational dynamics shape and plot the inner world of the psyche. Early family-of-origin experiences become internalized as personal maps of orientation, guiding persons in all subsequent interactions with the world and in their intimate relationships.

Patterns and Polarities

Therapies of the 1960s and 1970s targeted the family's destructive capacity to twist emotional and mental growth. Similarly, developmental psychology can highlight the deficits of the family environment. Some popular texts and television shows have depicted dysfunction in families as the constant in a vicious circle: "Dysfunctional families create dysfunctional individuals who marry other dysfunctional individuals and create new dysfunctional families" (Bradshaw, 1988, 62). Recovery movements for adult children of dysfunctional families have further dramatized the traumatic legacy of the dysfunctional family. By the 1980s, the field of therapy began to protest against this preoccupation with dysfunctional families. A current textbook in family systems theory cautions that the term *dysfunctional* "has taken on connotations of serious family disturbance and causal attributions that tend to overpathologize families and blame them for individual and social problems" (Walsh, 1993, 9).

The main problem with the concept of the dysfunctional family, however, is not the emphasis on its debilitating impact but the assumption that families *are* either functional or dysfunctional. Clinical experience demonstrates that there is no one way to profile either a healthy or sick family or differentiate the one from the other. Families cannot be reified into discrete entities but rather constitute centers of interpersonal interaction pulsing with multiple patterns and processes. Criteria of function and dysfunction relate to the *patterns* that organize family process. Rather than by intrinsic qualities, a pattern is deemed functional or dysfunctional by how it fits in a particular context or family situation. To add further complexity from a family systems perspective, a pattern may function well in one subsystem (e.g., parents being absorbed with a needy child), but dysfunction in other system levels such as sibling or marital relationships. Families express themselves through a multitude of diverse patterns, some functional, others dysfunctional, depending on the particular context.

In the *Circumplex Model* of couple and family systems, David Olson (1993) presents a conceptual design which proposes that family functioning is a matter of balancing polar opposites. The model is set up along two major dimensions. With the dimension of *cohesion* or emotional bonding, families need to balance separateness and togetherness. With the dimension of *flexibility* or the ability to adapt to change, families need to balance stability and transition. In describing family functioning, Olson uses the metaphor of skiing: "A professional skier smoothly shifts his or her weight from one leg to another, whereas a novice skier tends to emphasize one leg or another. In balanced families, people are able to move in a more fluid manner...whereas unbalanced systems tend to be stuck at one extreme or the other and have a difficult time shifting" (1993, 9). From this perspective, family health is not predicated by a finite list of required qualities and necessary conditions. Optimally healthy families practice the art of balancing the various polarities of life into infinite configurations that are unique and attuned to the constantly shifting terrain of their family in its developmental and cultural context.

A Family Vignette

In the British movie *Shirley Valentine*, based on Willy Russell's (1991) play, Shirley's husband Joe comes home one day from work to find a note pinned on the kitchen door: *Gone to Greece. Back in two weeks.* His wife has been persuaded by her girlfriend to go along on a vacation to Greece. While there Shirley reconnects with a part of herself that got lost in some twenty years of being a wife and a mother. The two-week vacation stretches into months, with no end in sight. The distraught husband is in crisis, feeling cheated, abandoned, and increasingly unable to function on his own in England. In spite of his ever more desperate phone calls and thoughts that she will be remembered by her children as "the mother who went on a holiday and never came back," Shirley holds on to her new life in Greece. With the family torn apart across continents, with all the symptoms of a typically "dysfunctional" family, the movie scripts a narrative where, to the contrary, Shirley emerges as the redemptive center of transformation, for herself as well as for her marriage and family.

The story tells Shirley's stretching from a rebellious schoolgirl to a devoted wife and mother. Her son and daughter, who have recently left home, are as yet loosely connected to the adult world. The daughter, with all her belongings stuffed in bags, returns to mother when conflict erupts with her roommate. Greece is part of an extended geography in Shirley's life. As a girl she was excited about the prospect of exploring the world but in school got the message that she would "never get far in life." She married early. We see Shirley and Joe as a young couple painting the kitchen walls. After a few playful spatters thrown at each other, a wild face-splashing chase ends up with both in the bathtub. Joe tells his wife: "A nut case you are. I love you Shirley Valentine." Over the years the couple settles in with work and family responsibilities. After launching their children, Shirley and Joe regroup as a couple, this time without the playfulness. Shirley says of her husband: "He loved me because I was a nut case, now he just thinks I am a nut case." Shirley begins to talk to the kitchen wall and drink white wine when she prepares dinner. A critical event occurs when Joe comes home and tea is not ready. Worse, it is Thursday and, rather than the customary steak, Shirley serves chips and egg—the Tuesday menu. Joe is enraged, screaming: "I think you are going around the bend." Shirley responds: "I hope so. I have always loved to travel." As routines and schedules constrain her in the kitchen, provoking the old adolescent rebelliousness, the wine beckons her to the land "where the grape is grown." On the inside of the kitchen closet, on a door straddling two worlds, is a large poster of Greece.

This family context gives Greece a meaning different from the one generated by a moralistic or individualistic focus on Shirley as a middle-aged "nut case" abandoning her marriage and family for a romantic adventure in the sun on an exotic island. The timing of this Greek "madness" links the children's leaving home with Shirley left in the confines of her kitchen. The presenting problem from a family life-cycle perspective is Shirley's being stuck in, rather than abandoning, her family. The movie ends with Joe and Shirley meeting again, this time not at the kitchen table but in Greece at a beach table with a bottle of wine. This final image leaves us with the paradox that the absence leads the way to a new presence. In the following section I propose a family assessment model that will evaluate families and couples not by a contents analysis of requirements for the functional family but by a process analysis of balancing competing claims under unique and taxing circumstances.

A Balanced Whole

From the perspective of the *Circumplex Model*, family and couple relationships operate in a tension-filled field of polarities. Polarities are made up of seeming contradictions, such as being absent *versus* being present or being on duty as opposed to being on vacation. Polarities, however, represent opposite ends that actually belong together and function as interdependent poles of "a balanced whole" (Tillich, 1951). Indeed, mounting strength at one polar end empowers the actualization of the opposite pole. In the Shirley

Valentine story, the marital separation facilitates a coming together in Greece, suggesting that initially it was the couple's togetherness that triggered the separation.

The circumplex model proposes that all the theoretical concepts that have been generated to describe family and couple dynamics can be represented in two dimensions: cohesion, and flexibility. A third dimension, communication, is not a separate domain but a facilitating condition for the other two dimensions. This chapter will expand the scope to seven polarities by incorporating the various perspectives of major family therapies.

The *integrity* and *accommodation* polarity relates to the family or couple **identity** and is basic to understanding systems functioning. This polarity holds a theology of life and death. Applied to the family, each pole in isolation represents one kind of death: the one the xenophobic extreme of *judgmental exclusiveness* by which the outer world is excluded, the "death of mere self-identity," the other the promiscuous extreme of *indiscriminate inclusiveness* by which the outer world overtakes the family or the couple, the "death of mere self-alteration" (Tillich, 1963). Systems can die by being either too closed or too open: two opposite styles of dysfunction and death. Relational and personal health occurs in the process of balancing these two poles: to secure an inner center *and* to engage outside influences and relationships that further define the center's essential identity and potential.

This first polarity plots the relational interactions by which the family or couple defines itself. This process identity can be further delineated by focusing on three areas of family functioning: its *political dynamic*, its *emotional system* and its *spiritual presence*. Each of these three domains, behavioral, emotional and spiritual, contains two sets of polarities.

The system's **political dynamic** relates to its structure and the use of power. Olson's *circumplex* model defines the power structure in terms of *family flexibility* as the amount of *change in its leadership, role relationships, and relationship rules*. The extreme polar opposites are *rigidity* (too much structure) and *chaos* (too little structure).

The Beavers (Beavers & Hampson, 1993) model of optimal family functioning describes the use of power as the overt expression of relatively equal power in the experience of intimacy. In order to avoid competitive tensions and conflicts, the Beavers model emphasizes the need for complementarity in the use of power that "encompasses difference, not an inferior/superior dynamic" (82). The extreme ends of this polarity are *coercion over others* and *undifferentiated symmetry*.

The concept of the **emotional system** stands out in the literature of family theory. The *Circumplex Model's* term *family cohesion* summarizes an abundance of theoretical terms describing emotional bonding among family members. Bowen's (Kerr & Bowen, 1988) biological theory of the *emotional system* describes the interplay of two counterbalancing life forces—*togetherness* and *individuality* in couple, family, and societal relationships. These two life forces, the one pushing toward *attachment*, the other pulling away in *separation*, constitute the two polar ends to be balanced in a relationship system. Bowen's core concept of *self-differentiation* points to a state of perfect balance, something we can aspire to though never fully achieve.

Salvador Minuchin (1974) graphically depicts family emotional connections through interpersonal *boundaries*: inappropriately rigid boundaries create *disengagement*, if boundaries are diffuse there is *enmeshment*. On the continuum between these two extremes is the mid-range of clear boundaries where family members can be close yet maintain a sense of personal identity and agency.

The concept of boundaries takes on special significance in family therapy when it applies to generational distinctiveness. Some of the most destructive family interactions take place in intergenerational alliances violating boundaries that protect the integrity and safety of children or the solidarity of the parental/marital relationship. Perverse triangles portray a parent-child alliance pitted against the other parent, often posing *split loyalty* (Boszormenyi-Nagy & Krasner, 1986) conflicts for the child where the love of the one parent comes at the cost of discounting the other. In contrast, when boundaries are overly restrictive and prohibitive, interpersonal connections are also impaired, often experienced in a sense of isolation and alienation.

A **spiritual presence** in the family is a more elusive concept in systems theory. It presupposes a belief system with significant transcendent values that emotionally charge and lend meaning to the life of the family and its members. This spiritual orientation becomes *present* in its functioning in the everyday interpersonal relationships of the family. Beavers describes the power of a caring and loving presence in optimal families: "Empathy for each other's feelings, interest in what each other has to say, and expectation of being understood encourage members to respond to each other with concern and action" (1993, 83). This sentence rightly balances giving care to others (empathy for feelings and interest in listening) with claiming care for self (expectation of being understood). These polar ends of responsibility toward others and rights for oneself are prominent in the theory of *Contextual Therapy*. It is the ethics of justice that seeks a balance between give and take, grounded in the interpersonal bond of covenant trustworthiness.

The psychoanalytic theory of *Self Psychology* (Kohut, 1971, 1977, Elson, 1986) proposes a polar structure for the self in relationship with a significant other. Kohut (1971) developed a double axis theory based on two reciprocal human relational needs: 1) to be affirmed by significant others as special, and 2) to have a significant one to admire and take comfort in. These two poles constitute the *bipolar self*. These two relational needs stand out in early childhood when the child strives for recognition and looks to the parent as an object to be idealized and imitated. In a perfect family scenario the child's grandiose self is transformed into healthy ambitions and the idealized parent is internalized as ideals and values. In reality the two polar needs are never fully satisfied, not even under the best circumstances, but persist through time. This is demonstrated when others continue to be recruited in our lives as *selfobjects*, to perform the ongoing functions of *mirroring* (validating the self) and *idealizing* (soothing the self).

This polar structure of the self accentuates the spiritual dimension in human nature. The need to idealize points to the need to transcend one's individual identity and limitations and merge with someone or something larger than the self to comfort as well as to inspire and guide. The need for mirroring is the need to be blessed and confirmed in one's special giftedness, purpose, and vocation in life. Idealizing and mirroring are relational pathways towards a *cohesive self* (Kohut, 1971) and a meaningful place in the world. Ideally both idealizing and mirroring are present, but in the absence of one the other can still facilitate the development of the self. When these two relational needs are arranged as polar ends—one assigning greatness to the self, the other assigning greatness to the other—the potential for to make one or the other absolute becomes apparent. In the context of the family there is the possibility of the extremes of either a *family clan*, where the ethnocentric ideals, values, history or religion of the family become the dominant reality, or a *person cult*, where the narcissistic needs and aspirations of the star of the family or the claims of privileged status of a family member structure the family.

Table 8.1   Core Dimensions of Family Functioning

Focus	Polarity	Extremes		Principle
Family: •identity	1. integrity and accommodation	judgmental exclusiveness	indiscriminate inclusiveness	family/couple definition
•political dynamic	2. structure and flexibility	rigidity in roles and rules	chaos in rules and leadership	system change
	3. power and equality	coercive control over others	undifferentiated symmetry	relationship intimacy
•emotional system	4. attachment and separateness	clinging and dependency	reactiveness and disengagement	self differentiation
	5. affiliation and boundaries	triangles and split loyalties	isolation and alienation	generation distinctiveness
•spiritual presence	6. responsibilities and rights	no caring for self	no caring for others	covenant trustworthiness
	7. idealizing and mirroring	a family clan	a person cult	vocation confirmation

Applications

The *Core Dimensions of Family Functioning* (CDFF) diagram is intended as an internal map of orientation for the counselor, a safeguard against dogmatic, limiting, and pathologizing extremes in therapy. Further, the CDFF table, can become a psychoeducational assessment tool to be shared with families and couples as a discussion guide. If Shirley Valentine, alone or with Joe, would present for therapy, the CDFF diagram would signal a variety of issues to be pursued in exploratory and affirmative conversations. In letting the diagram outline draw the therapy map, the following issues present themselves:

1. **Identity:** Shirley married young, before she had time to establish a cohesive sense of herself. Her personal identity merged prematurely with the marriage and, soon after, a family. Her family involvement included the loss of personal friends except the one girlfriend, significantly a person who had been recently divorced and was in search of a new life. The family has launched the two children. With the children gone, Shirley finds that the marriage is also gone. In terms of the identity polarity, the extreme of exclusive family involvement raises the urgency of connecting with a world beyond the kitchen door.

2. **Political Dynamic:** The story accentuates a rigid structure dramatized in oppressive rules about when to drink tea and what to eat on what day. When Shirley changes the menu she faces Joe's outrage. There is a parallel reality with Joe—running his shop is a harrowing and isolating experience for him. Joe and Shirley come across as two disempowered people, the one confined in the shop, the other in the kitchen. In sharing their powerlessness, their intimacy gets lost in an escalating struggle for personal control.

3. **Emotional System:** Shirley becomes aware as her children leave home that she herself has never left home. Greece is the symbol of a world she has never known and that now beckons her. The story of the two children dramatizes the polar ends of attachment and separation. The daughter, even though gone, still clings to her mother and readily regresses to child dependency. She is enraged when her mother is leaving, and in her feeling of abandonment she allies with her father in insisting that Shirley's role is to be the caretaker at home. In contrast to his younger sister, the son *has* left home and relates to his parents as fellow adults. He confronts the father for living a boring life, tied to a small world of work and home, not able to meet his wife in a new world. In this sibling story, clear boundaries and strength of self-differentiation are contrasted with emotional triangles.

4. **Spiritual Presence:** Shirley acts out the anger of grieving the losses that have accumulated over the years. It starts with telling Joe to go away and read the paper when there is no tea and dinner is late. The episode foreshadows that she will not just be late, but not be there at all. In the movie the absence of

tea progresses to an absent steak and culminates in an absent Shirley. The couple's covenant arrangement and trust is broken. The balance of caring has been too long in favor of Joe and the family. In addressing the imbalance, Shirley is drawn into an extreme position: claiming her own life at the cost of her marriage and family.

Shirley has been loyally serving the needs of her family for over twenty years, yet she has gained no personal affirmation and recognition. Her story illustrates the feminist critique that women have been assigned the one-way vocation of being there for others. In Greece she enjoys a brief romantic interaction, meets people, makes friends and finds a job. Greece symbolizes that Shirley has found her place in the world. Greece also signifies the place where Joe and Shirley need to meet if there is to be a new beginning and a new life for them as a couple and as a family.

Conclusion

The CDFF diagram posits seven principles of family health:

- Authenticity in defining oneself as a family
- Adaptability in redefining oneself as a family
- Enjoyment of interpersonal intimacy in the family
- Freedom for individual self-differentiation
- Security for children through family boundaries
- Mutual trustworthiness in family relations
- Power to bless the child and each other

The healthy family pursues these values in a lifetime of balancing the respective polar ends of the above principles. This approach acknowledges the constantly shifting terrain that families and family members need to negotiate when defining themselves in their daily lives and highlights the following main characteristics:

- It is multi-perspectival by incorporating diverse viewpoints in a comprehensive framework, informed by the wisdom of essential family theories.

- It is process directed in its focus not on a content analysis but on the tensions and shifts in family interactions within the larger picture of the family in its developmental process and cultural context.

- It is health oriented by its emphasis that potentially pathological extremes can be part of the family's resilience and wisdom in re-establishing its balance.

- It is spirituality informed by its therapeutic aim to resolve polarized extremes and impasses into a process of transformation and by its theology of health as a balancing act sustained by the hope and vision of moving towards a "balanced whole."

CHAPTER 9

▨ Textures and Threads:
Life Cycle Transitions

MRS BERG ARRIVED TO SEE a pastoral counselor in a state of depression. She located the onset of her distress in her daughter's recent departure from home to stay with a favorite aunt and her family some 500 kilometers away. The move was intended as time out in countering runaway escalation of family stress at home. Mrs Berg had provided the main impetus for getting her 16-year-old daughter out of the house—something that now flooded her with feelings of guilt and regret.

The mother-daughter relationship had been severely conflicted for at least the last two years. The memory of an especially ugly fight on the eve of her daughter's departure had become an obsession in the mother's mind. In sharp contrast, her husband could look back on a largely pleasant, often playful, relationship with his daughter. The mother was left isolated and resentful in losing a daughter from whom she felt now separated not only relationally but also geographically. She was grieving a double loss, both parts of which stemmed from her sense of failure as a parent.

Family Togetherness

While family theorists have uniformly stressed that healthy families balance connectedness with separateness (Kerr & Bowen, 1988), North American society often cherishes the romantic ideal that families can never be close enough. Family systems theory presents a more playful, if not turbulent, profile of the functional family, with the two polar ends on the togetherness continuum in constant interaction for an optimal balance to fit the family developmental needs in its specific situation. (Olson, 1993; Beavers & Hampson, 1993). Families with young children generally gravitate toward close and protective family boundaries, while at least in the Western world, families with adolescents often need to relax their boundaries to permit movement, at times collisions, between parents and the expanding world of the adolescent.

The Berg family experiences opposite claims in structuring the family. With two children at different ages, a 9-year-old boy and a 16-year-old girl, the family is at different points in the family life cycle. The traditional gender assumption that girls need more family protection than boys may further complicate the confusion in the family. At this critical juncture in the family life cycle, the daughter has the daunting task to redefine the family constellation and initiate disorienting family interactions. The family togetherness that was functional before has now become dysfunctional.

The Bowen school of family systems theory offers an enlightening perspective on family togetherness (Kerr & Bowen, 1988, 59-111). It states that rather than opposite ends on a togetherness continuum, family disengagement and family enmeshment are actually two sides of the same coin. Both stem from "emotional fusion" that is expressed in two different styles: one in clinging together at all cost, the other in reactivity and, in the extreme, through emotional cutoffs. The opposite of emotional fusion is not separation but "self-differentiation"—i.e. the ability to establish a self while emotionally connected with and actively participating in the family. According to this view, the long geographical distance between mother and daughter in the Berg family does not amount to one centimeter of psychological distance. From the Bowen perspective, the problem is not the distance but the closeness: the daughter's departure only accentuates her pivotal location in the emotional system of the family, exacerbating the feelings of distress.

Role Differentiation

This chapter incorporates the *genogram* (see Appendix 3) as a graphic representation of the family as an emotional system moving through space and time over at least three generations (McGoldrick & Gerson, 1985; Carter & McGoldrick, 1999). The genogram maps recurring behavioral patterns and emotional ties among family members. The genogram has become a standard assessment tool for a systemic approach in therapy and is generally shared with the couple or family. Presenting problems lose their narrow focus on the individual when they begin to tell the story of the family. The genogram differentiates the various roles by which the person participates in the family system. Mrs Berg has identified the problem in her perceived personal failure as a mother relating to a daughter with an attitude. The genogram, however, also casts Mrs Berg in many other roles, including daughter, wife, co-parent, sister, and in-law. Such a contextual approach in therapy clears new space where the presenting problem can be explored in less contaminated settings.

According to the genogram in Figure 9.1, Mrs Berg is the oldest of five children in her family of origin. Not only being the first born, but also the untimely death of the second child, distanced Mrs Berg from her younger siblings and accentuated her care-taking role as the *parental child* in the family. She was close to her mother, the primary parent in spite of some thirty hours per week she worked outside the home as a cleaning lady. The father was a quiet, unobtrusive man, the night clerk in the local hotel, and largely peripheral to the day-to-day events in his own family. Mrs Berg's next younger sister is the only sibling who attended university. She has established a lifestyle of her own, often at variance from the more conventional values in the family of origin, presently living in a committed lesbian relationship with the child from her partner's previous relationship. The youngest sister had a car accident in her early teens, which has left her with some mental impairment. She lives at home with her mother. Their brother has moved from the east to the west coast from where he maintains pleasant but sporadic contacts with the family.

Mrs Berg has a long history of being close to her mother. In the family of origin the mother depended on Mrs Berg as a co-parent, especially when she was working outside the home. Mrs Berg still receives frequent calls from her mother, often related to her youngest sister who at the age of 34 continues to require emotional and practical support. In exploring the relationship with her mother, Mrs Berg became aware how limited her experience had been of being a "daughter" or a "child." With her mother coping with long hours and functioning virtually as a "single" parent, Mrs Berg was prematurely recruited as co-parent in a large family.

The genogram opens multiple possibilities and avenues for therapy. From a family systems perspective, a presenting problem can be approached from different directions since the problem is not localized in and confined to where it presents itself in the family. At times, as in the case of Mrs Berg, a presenting problem is so emotionally charged that it needs to be addressed somewhere else in the family system to allow a space for therapy to take place. In differentiating Mrs Berg's roles in the family system, defocusing the overworked mother role, family therapy can focus on other relational locales in the genogram such as Mrs Berg's relationship with her own mother or her relationship with her husband. The related systems concepts (Von Bertalanffy, 1968) of *isomorphism* (the commonality of shape and process between the various subsystems of a system) and *equifinality* (that similar outcomes can result from different origins) mean in family therapy that choosing the place of therapy intervention is a matter of clinical expediency. The case study here illustrates that marital therapy often becomes the treatment of choice for parenting problems.

Couple Therapy

Couple therapy focuses on the role differentiation present in the couple/marital subsystem within the multi-generational family system. Mrs Berg's family of origin is connected with Mr Berg's family of origin in their shared genogram (Figure 9.1). In his family of origin, Mr Berg is the youngest child with two older sisters. His father, after a long and lingering illness, died when he was 5 years old. His oldest sister, apparently feeling displaced by her more glamorous younger sister, the star of the family, early on distanced herself from the family, culminating in her immigration to Australia. Mr Berg grew up as a carefree child, much doted on as the baby of the family by both his mother and his next older sister. Not surprising, he married another "older sister," and continued a congenial and pleasant existence, working part-time as a music teacher in the town's high school, while owning a rental store specializing in musical instruments and gardening and building equipment.

Figure 9.1   The Berg Genogram

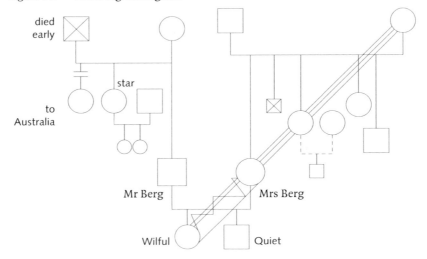

Couple relationships generally work in a complementary fashion. In the Berg couple economy, Mrs Berg does most of the worrying: she takes responsibility as primary parent, homemaker, and the bookkeeper of the store. Mr Berg does most of the pleasing and contributes to a comfortable atmosphere in the home and in their social relationships.

Having initiated couple therapy, the couple describes their relationship as a balancing act between Mrs Berg "the pessimist" and Mr Berg "the optimist." In this arrangement it makes sense that in addressing their family crisis, Mrs Berg is assigned the task of being the *identified patient* with the presenting problem of "depression." The therapist expresses her surprise and admiration that as a couple they can appreciate and coordinate their differences rather than fight about them. The complementarity also rules their parenting system, with a mother who disciplines and a father who charms. The therapist notes that being an adolescent is so hard because you need to push parents away yet feel close and supported by them, and says: "I am impressed by your shared arrangement that makes it possible for your daughter to both fight and play with her parents. What I feel sad about is that you, Mrs Berg, got the more difficult and thankless job of doing the fighting. The trouble with task divisions is that it makes you an expert in just one thing."

In further sessions the Bergs design and practice role reversals. In owning shared stress they plan a short vacation trip. According to their customary marital role division, Mrs Berg would assume the task of travel guide in organizing the trip. In a role reversal scenario, Mr Berg takes on the responsibility of securing information from the travel agency and arranging adequate funds for their vacation. Mrs Berg practices the art of a carefree attitude and having a good time. In a second role reversal plan, Mr Berg will, upon his daughter's return, negotiate a reasonable budget with her and be strict in distributing a monthly allowance within clear guidelines. Mrs Berg will look for time to share with her daughter in more fun-related activities such as aerobic exercises.

The Time Perspective

The time perspective, which relates problems to the flow of stress through the family and how it is addressed in the process of family coping, takes on special relevance in couple and family therapy. Therapists have long noted that presenting problems often coincide with critical transition points in the family life cycle (Haley, 1973). Problems can take on a life of their own as distinct entities rather than remaining the signals that punctuate critical moments in the life cycle. Families and couples who are aware of this can see the normalcy of an experience that may appear lethal and terminal. Carter and McGoldrick aptly observe: "Families characteristically lack time perspective when they are having problems. They tend generally to magnify the present moment, overwhelmed and immobilized by their immediate feelings; or they become fixed on a moment in the future that they dread or long for. They lose the awareness that life means continual motion from the past into the future with a continual transformation of familial relationships" (1999, 4).

Life cycle transitions shift the state of family relationships and require a repositioning in the dynamics of the couple relationship. This is the "emotional process" (Kerr & Bowen, 1988) by which the family regulates the balance between individuality and togetherness, the dance between contraction and expansion in the evolution of family relationships. The adolescent daughter in the Berg family triggers the life cycle transition that throws the family system out of balance. In cultures that value individual autonomy, adolescents often instigate the signals for the family to open its boundaries and permit freer movement between the family and its surrounding world. Such shifts generally require radical reorganization and redefinition of the family. It is not surprising that these transitions bring high levels of stress and anxiety that challenge the couple as the family's chief executive team. It makes both clinical and ethical sense to designate couple relationship as the party responsible to negotiate and validate family life cycle shifts.

The time perspective links problems of the family coping process with life stressors. Stress is an inherent part of family life and successful families engage rather than avoid the stress in their lives. Some stressors, such as life cycle and migration transitions, are predictable and normative, while others are unpredictable, catastrophic events, such as untimely death, accidents, unemployment, natural disasters, and war. In his classic research study of postwar families in the 1940s, Reuben Hill (1949) identified two crucial factors in the family process of coping with stress: 1) the family resources, and 2) the family's definition and interpretation of the stress. Subsequent family stress theory has refined Hill's original conceptual model, but the twofold formula of coping with stress through the process of interacting resources and interpretations has remained a helpful paradigm (Figley & McCubbin, 1983; Burr & Klein, 1994). From this perspective, family stress arises from an actual or perceived imbalance between the demands of life and the family's ability to meet these demands and transform them into positive outcomes. This definition comes to life when applied to the story of the Berg family. The twofold coping process is evident in their utilization of *family resources* and *family interpretation*.

The Bergs's use of family resources is apparent in the following:

- The integrity of the marital system. Rather than a divisive triangle formation with a benevolent father aligning with the daughter against a demanding wife/mother, the couple maintains mutual loyalty and addresses the need for change first in their own relational system.
- The extended family. A safety net of extended family relations provides temporary respite to both daughter and mother.
- The openness in mobilizing extra-familial resources through therapy.
- Financial resources generated by the couple, evident in resettling the daughter and in the couple's re-connecting and re-grouping as a couple on their vacation trip.

Active family interpretation appears in the following therapeutic shifts:

- Initial definition of the problem used individual terms and pathology labels: it targeted the daughter as the problem and the mother as the victim/patient in need of treatment. A psychoeducational approach in therapy through the family life cycle saw the situation as normal family stress and validated the integrity and power of the marital relationship.
- The role differentiation approach provided new perspectives that involved a less-stigmatized mother role.

Family transition stress, though painful and disruptive, provides the impetus for couples to change and regulate the development of their own marital life cycle (Nichols, 1988, 17-39). Mrs Berg as the family's symptom-bearer identifies the need for the family to rethink, redefine, and restructure itself. Such a transition point requires the timing of stress at a crisis level. From a family system perspective, a crisis is a state of family disorganization that demands a change in its very structure of being and doing things. The restructuring and redefinition of the marital relationship in the Berg family is the therapeutic goal in restoring balance in the family.

Dimensions of Structural Change

Changing the family system requires a change at the structural level, often best achieved by addressing the couple and/or parental subsystems. As their names express, that is the goal in both structural and constructivist therapies. Structural family therapy is associated with the work of Minuchin (1974), and describes the internal organization of subsystems and boundaries of a family and how these define interactional patterns and behavior. Structural therapy concerns the structure of relational systems such as redrawing interpersonal boundaries or practicing role reversals as recounted in the Berg couple therapy sessions. Constructivist therapy holds that human beings are meaning-making creatures who construct out of their lived experience the realities they live by. Constructivist therapy invites people into dialogue, and uses shared personal stories to jointly assess, deconstruct or reconstruct old meanings and create new meanings (Rosen & Kuehlwein, 1996). Adapting a Carter & McGoldrick (1999, 6) diagram, Figure 9.2 depicts the horizontal time dimension of stress as it flows through the family and intersects with a vertical dimension of prior experiences and meanings that inform the process by which family members interpret the stressors. Constructivist theory holds that meaning-making constructs exist on many levels—individual, marital, familial, social, religious, and cultural—that conjointly determine the meaning a person attributes to stress events.

Transgenerational family therapies (Roberto, 1992) see the family as a meaning-making culture active in constructing a family reality—a reality that is maintained in family stories, myths, and legacies, and through emotional and relational patterns in triangles, alliances, rules, and expectations. Families are embedded in larger sociocultural meaning-making cultures articulated in beliefs, attitudes, and prejudices on such life issues as power, sexuality, gender, race and ethnicity, success and failure, and religious values. Carter and McGoldrick (1999) largely restrict this vertical meaning-making dimension to a stress-provoking dynamic, speaking of "horizontal" and "vertical" stressors that in conjunction make for "a quantum leap in anxiety in the system" (1999, 7).

In therapy with the Berg couple, the "vertical" line of a tradition of strong women in correlation with decent but rather passive men became apparent. The stress impact of this tradition of women responsible for managing their families probably increased the level of anxiety in the family's emotional system when Mrs Berg increasingly felt unable to meet this legacy. The counseling, however, saw this same tradition, as positive by interpreting the daughter's wilfulness as a sign of strength of character: she is able to stand up to her mother, something that Mrs Berg had trouble doing with her own mother.

An example of horizontal stress intersecting with vertical stress-inducing history in the Berg family relates to emotional cutoffs of daughters and their families. Emotional cutoff is a Bowen concept that describes the way family members manage the emotional intensity and lack of differentiation between them and between the generations (Kerr & Bowen, 1988, 271ff). In Mr Berg's family of origin this happened with the oldest daughter who both geographically and psychologically left for another continent. This cutoff has been compensated for by the younger daughter who maintains a double presence in the family, and who also at this point in time substitutes by providing a home away from home for the Berg daughter. In Mrs Berg's family of origin a complicating piece of family history that may contribute to the present crisis, is the experience of a lost child in the untimely death of her brother.

Figure 9.2   The Coping Process

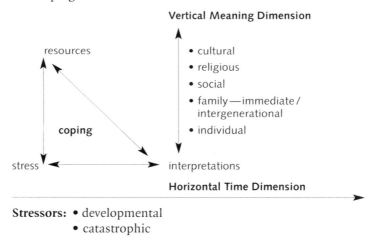

Vertical Meaning Dimension

resources

• cultural
• religious
• social
• family—immediate /
  intergenerational
• individual

coping

stress   interpretations

Horizontal Time Dimension

Stressors: • developmental
• catastrophic

Dimensions of Transformation

The process of interpretation in constructivist therapy is crucial in the practice of spiritual care and therapy. The process of interpretation provokes new meanings and constructs alternative personal and family realities. These shifts in perspective translate into basic life changes. Family theory distinguishes three levels of change:

1. **Level 1** change is defined as change within the family system that does not alter its basic structure (Watzlawick, Weakland & Fisch, 1974). In the Berg family, a level 1 change is negotiated when the daughter leaves to live with her aunt and family. This change maintains the structural parts of the marriage, the family and the larger extended family such as the substitute role of the aunt. Even though it is probably a helpful change, providing a pause

in escalating conflict, it does not change the fundamental patterns of organization in the system.

2 **Level 2** change, better known as "second-order" change, impacts the structure of the system itself (Watzlawick, Weakland & Fisch, 1974). In counseling the Berg couple, the structural intervention of role reversals addresses fundamental rules that pattern their interaction, such as the polarity between Mrs Berg's over-responsible and Mr Berg's under-responsible stances. The goal of level 2 change is not to change something in the system but to change the system itself.

3 **Level 3** change is the most radical change as it affects basic life orientations (Reiss, 1981). Beyond the family system it refers to one's place in the world. level 3 change is a shift in paradigms, in the basic beliefs and assumptions about life. There are many stories of radical change in human life, transformations that currently are researched and identified as instances of "quantum change" (Miller & C'de Baca, 2001). At moments of severe stress a person or, to stay with the Berg family, a couple may go through a transforming experience similar to a life-changing spiritual conversion. The closest example in the case study is the personal life reorientation in Mrs Berg. She begins to question the meaning of responsibility and caretaking—core values that have organized her life, robbed her from her childhood, and let her down in a crisis of mounting family stress. Repositioning herself in the family as a whole person not confined to the parent role, calls for a systems conversion where the marriage redefines itself and moves into new life. Such a change in the context of couple therapy will involve a parallel process in Mr Berg as he critically assesses his own placating strategy (Satir, 1988, 85) in adapting to the problems of life and his family stress.

Change theory clarifies that life cycle transitions are generally second-, at rare and special times, third-order changes. Radical change involves both role differentiation and time perspective. Role differentiation is a reorientation in *space*: how persons situate themselves in the structure of their intimate relationships and in their world. Life cycle perspectives facilitate a reorientation in *time*: how persons envision their lives flowing from the past into the future, inviting continual transformation by reframing problems into challenges.

Constructivist and narrative theories believe that life transformations are generated through therapeutic conversations that explore and construct new meanings. Third-order change is an ambitious goal: seeking to integrate time and space dimensions in the creation of new structures of meaning. As Anderson and Worthen outline this process in an article on spirituality as a resource in couple therapy:

> Three dimensions of experience addressed by most therapies are time (events occurring in sequences), space (experience organized through the structure of relationships), and story (the use of language to shape what has occurred in

time and space into structures of meaning). The latter includes stories told inside our heads, stories told to others with whom we interact in time and space, stories that families construct and pass on over generations, and stories constructed by societies and cultures. (1997, 3)

Meaning-construction is a process of integration, and in the context of the Bergs, includes structural family therapy (the space dimension of therapy) and life cycle and transgenerational therapy (the time perspective). It is the integration of concrete experience grounded in present relationships and the more abstract experience of movement through time toward the revisioning of life into the future.

Conclusion

Spiritual care and family therapy may present as an "odd couple," but from a constructivist/narrative perspective, the couple is not to be divorced. A couple's relationship is guided by their joined narratives, a "conjugal mythology" (Bargarozzi & Anderson, 1989, 77). A spiritual approach looks at the personal and communal stories of meaning and faith people live by and share with intimate others. Spiritual care has a special entrée and vocation in attending to these stories by co-interpreting and, at times, co-scripting alternative visions of life and rituals of transition (see chapter 11). Human transformation becomes profoundly spiritual when relational systems and the meanings of life are seen in an integrative and liberating perspective.

CHAPTER 10

Endings and Beginnings: Crisis and Loss

AT THE AGE OF 28, Maria suddenly became a widow when her husband John, at 50, died of a heart attack. An immigrant from Greece, John had come to Canada in his early thirties. After ten years of hard work in construction, culminating in building his own house, he returned to his native country to marry a young woman from the village where he grew up. He brought his bride, Maria, to Canada where in another year their son was born. John's unexpected and untimely death left Maria reeling, lonely, and abandoned in a strange land to which she felt bound through her 6-year-old son.

Maria became one of my first clients when I enrolled in a clinical education program some thirty years ago. My main source of information about the grieving process came from Kübler-Ross's *On Death and Dying* (1969), at the time an immensely popular book. It proposed a progression of stages by which terminal patients deal with their impending death: from denial, anger, bargaining, and depression to, when all goes well, final acceptance. These same stages were generally applied to the grief experience of those facing not their own death but the death of a loved one—often entailing the experience of losing a part of themselves.

A death marks a family life cycle transition. Some deaths are predictable, can even mark a time of celebration when death crowns a life well and fully lived. Other deaths in the family are a horror, a catastrophic event—untimely, sudden and violent, tearing the textures that nest the family and unraveling the threads of continuity. Such transitions are cut with endings that require, if life is to continue, new beginnings.

Maria's priest referred her to counseling after such a death. It was a full week after her husband's funeral and she was in a state of shock, in the rawness of acute pain, unable to grasp the enormity of her loss. John had been much more to her than a husband. As a prince, he had come to take her from her little village to a big and exciting world where he had built a house for her. A father figure, he took care of everything—from looking after the bills to getting the groceries—her only link to the world outside the home. Maria asked me: "Will I ever be able to mention his name, or look at his picture, without feeling this terrible pain?"

I remember the startling shift when Maria's adoration of John turned to anger. As a student therapist I experimented with the *Gestalt* technique of the "empty chair," asking Maria to face John in the other chair. Soon Maria began to confront John with her "unfinished business." Her rage surfaced: he had cut her off from her own people only to desert her now in a foreign land, and left her with a son, also called John, to keep her from returning home.

Eventually the anger led to moments of sadness and a sobering realization that she was now on her own in new territory. Maria began to plan for her own and her son's survival: she explored her financial situation, decided to get her driver's license and enroll in a course in English. She began her psychological immigration to Canada. By mutual planning we moved toward terminating the counseling as she became increasingly involved in her new life. Rather than just recovering from grief, Maria redefined herself, starting her own immigrant story.

Some counseling clients seem to stay with you long after the counseling ends. Having witnessed her grieving process taking her towards the thrust of new life, memories of Maria often join me as I see other clients. At the time it felt like a mysterious process, something much larger than either Maria or the counseling. I perceived Kübler-Ross's theory as a glimpse into a grand, universal design, a preordained process of therapeutic stages to be trusted as we grieve our losses. Through the years I have revisited Maria's experience from different theoretical perspectives to compose a larger and more diversified picture. This chapter will highlight two perspectives: 1) the family system as the relational context that shapes each individual family member's grief experience, and 2) the hermeneutical task of constructing a healing theory and new meanings to live by.

The Family Context

A family systems perspective sees individual grief experiences as interdependent parts that interact within the larger context of the family dynamic. That is the original meaning of the word system: a complex of interacting elements. From this systems perspective on grief, three levels of family organization can be distinguished (VanKatwyk, 1993), dimensions that can be placed on a continuum of increasing differentiation between the family and its individual members:

1. the *bio-physical*
2. the *psycho-social*
3. the *spiritual-vocational*

A family's initial grief reactions often are overwhelmingly physical. Grief manifests at the very bodily foundation of our being. Erich Lindemann's research (1944) with survivors of the Coconut Grove night club fire in Boston emphasized somatic distress in grief, what seems like the body's protest to the loss of the deceased family member through sensory distortions, including auditory and visual hallucinations. The most basic level of the family context is the concrete, *bio-physical* expressions of family life. Developmentally this is the way each person is initiated into life. At birth the infant appears to be sensitive only to bodily functions and bodily contacts, the physical comfort and/or deprivation experiences between the infant and the care taking family presence. The home environment uniquely retains this grounding in the body and in providing a sense of basic security in later developmental stages.

Family therapists often ask about their clients' home situation, including its physical outlay, whether doors are left open or closed, the morning rituals when the family gets up for a new day, the routines around the use of the bathroom and breakfast in the kitchen. All of this forms a sensual texture holding a person's life. When a family member dies, this physical texture that holds our life is torn apart. Grief includes this sense of physical dislocation and lostness. There is the empty chair, the sudden silence, an aching sense of sensory deprivation in no longer being able to see and touch the deceased family member. When a car stops, there is no follow-up response at the backdoor. The sound of voice and feet coming down the staircase no longer mark the beginning of a new day. The family as a mystical union is symbolised by the one *home* with its various sacraments and ritual activities that punctuate the family experience and gather its members into the one-flesh union of the family body.

Murray Bowen developed a scale of levels in self-differentiation (Kerr & Bowen, 1988, 97-107). Families with little self-differentiation among their members feel "fused" and are described as "closed." These families identify themselves by high levels of anxiety and emotional reactivity when their shared identity and common experience as a family is threatened. The level of self-differentiation is commonly experienced as a flexible continuum. In times of stress and crisis, such as in the real or anticipated loss of a family member, individuals generally regress on the scale of self-differentiation and experience anxieties and overwhelming feelings of helplessness in the face of impending disintegration. These feelings are part of acute grief reactions and most directly manifest themselves through the body.

The initial emotional shock that registers somatically is followed by more complex interpersonal reactions. The *psycho-social* context for grief is found in the family as a covenantal community where individual family members reciprocally define the family as the context for each member's individual identity. While family members are differentiated through the generational hierarchy and specific position in the family, individual roles and functions serve primarily the needs of the family in maintaining its corporate identity and emotional homeostasis.

This family socialization process is central in infancy and early adolescence. Daniel Stern, in his influential research study, *The Interpersonal World of the Infant*, states that already at the age of two to three months, "the infant's first order of business, in creating an interpersonal world, is to form the sense of a core self and core others" (1985, 70). The family as an interpersonal system consists of persons who perform interdependent social roles and psychological functions that provide each member, and the family as a whole, with an identity.

Some roles are common to most families, among them: mother, stepdad, child, older sister, baby brother, visiting uncle, grandmother, and close household friend. Families also tend to have special vocations to which family members are called such as mentors, clowns, chaplains, patients, and stars. Family roles often follow complementary patterns such as leaders and followers, peace-disturbers and peace-makers, saints and sinners. Once recruited into such functions, each person stabilizes the family system and confirms the individual roles of respective family members. The covenant concept conveys this contractual structure of relational roles, rules, and obligations that define each person's identity in reciprocal, interpersonal terms.

The psychoanalytic theory, *object relations* (Greenberg & Mitchell, 1983; Mitchell, 1988; Slipp, 1984), describes how each person carries the configuration of interpersonal family roles and relationship patterns experienced as a child. This inner family becomes a template for subsequent relationships and the context for self-identity and personal awareness. In case of a death in the family, the so-called "surviving" family members are at risk of losing themselves. Bowen discusses that a death in the family is largely defined by the special function of the deceased individual in the family system (1991, 79-93). The death of the main caregiver in a family of dependent members, or the death of a young child who carries the joys and hopes of the family, is likely to be followed by major family disruption.

A third dimension in the family's constellation is the distinct and unique place of the individual in the family. This focus on individual autonomy in Western culture gains prominence in adolescence when individual identity needs to be balanced with family loyalties and interpersonal connections. Psychology theories often highlight this developmental task as the supreme goal for the actualization of human wholeness. It is the movement from an identity primarily constituted by the performance of certain social roles and psychological functions for others in the family to a sense of self clearly differentiated from others. It takes a certain moral capacity and psychological maturity for the family to see its members both as family members and as distinct from the configuration of family expectations and needs. The covenantal structure of the family now transcends its own interests and survival. The covenant of contractual obligations becomes secondary to a covenant of grace. Identity is now found primarily in the personal experience of acceptance and confirmation. Intimacy is now experienced in the interpersonal interaction of knowing and being known.

Jewish philosopher Martin Buber (1965) focused on confirming the other as the most significant feature of all human interaction. It is the mark of the true humanness of a society and the healthy family. Rather than being determined by the "family script" or being enlisted into the service of family needs and ambitions, family members experience permission to define a self. Such a family environment affords personal validation and acknowledgment. In authentic personal encounters a person is grasped yet respected. It is a moment of revelation, sometimes in a flash of mutual recognition. Such moments of seeing and mirroring each other constitute the sacred history of the family. These moments are often reflected in a collection of special letters, photo albums, and family stories, illustrating family interaction with snapshots of discovery and recognition. From this perspective, the spiritual vocation of the family is to transcend its own identity as a family clan and confirm the integrity and vocation of its individual members.

The Family Story

What happens with the family story after a death in the family? How does the family continue when a main character is gone? At the core of the grieving process is the question how life can continue: "What do we do now?" Traditional psychoanalytic bereavement models emphasized that successful grieving means to relinquish one's attachment to the deceased person and reinvest one's life and energy into somebody or something else. In this way the family story continues through replacing what has been lost.

With the death of a child, the search for replacement can put other siblings at risk. Says William Worden in a chapter on *grief and family systems*: "One of the most difficult positions parents put the surviving siblings in is to be the substitute for the lost child. This often involves endowing the survivor-child with qualities of the deceased" (1991, 120, 121). In contrast to replacement, a family systems perspective proposes the creation of a new and enduring relationship with the deceased family member. It is a more humane view than the theory that we can shift human beings as interchangeable love objects. As summarized by Ester Shapiro:

> A systemic developmental perspective on adult bereavement suggests that the end point of successful grief work is not relinquishment of the lost relationship but the creation of a new bond, one that acknowledges the enduring psychological and spiritual reality of someone we have loved and made a part of ourselves. In this culture we have a difficult time granting even to children the need to retain an enduring bond with the dead, so determined are we to promote the reality-oriented "letting go" process. Yet both children and adults require the security and safety provided by the spiritual and emotional presence of their important formative attachment figures. (1994, 41-42)

The concept of *relocation* is perhaps the best way to describe this view of family grieving. This term acknowledges the sense of defiance in refusing to give up the dead person for dead. The dynamics of *replacement* focuses on re-establishing one's own place in life to continue one's story. Relocation, rather than replacement, establishes a place for the dead person, without letting that place get into the way of ongoing life. This approach holds on to the ongoing life of the deceased family member even though acknowledging the reality of the person's death. It is found in the search to locate the meaning of the person who has died, to grasp and be grasped by the living memories of the dead, and to incorporate within one's own life and family circle the living essence of the other. Maria did not choose to continue her life by replacing Canada by Greece, the older John by the younger John, or marriage by therapy. Through relocation her husband stayed present for her as a migration symbol: the courage to re-story one's life in unfamiliar and trying circumstances. This living legacy of her husband challenged her to begin her own immigrant story.[1]

Beyond the immediate urgency of surviving the trauma of catastrophic loss of life, there is the task to incorporate the death in the family story. At this point the focus is less on feelings than on thoughts in the grieving process. In this grief work, the death is transformed by a healing perspective through which the deceased family member participates in the ongoing life of the family and its members. In this approach the question of meaning stands central, with a special urgency for those cases of loss that appear to be singularly brutal and senseless.

Summary and Discussion

These reflections, shaped by systemic and constructivist perspectives, contrast at points with traditional stage theories of the grief experience. From the above case example we can draw a profile with the following interrelated concepts:

1. **A death is always a family event**
   In family systems theory, death is an integral part of the family life cycle. Rather than focus on individual grief reactions and attending perils or

---

1 Such grief work belongs to the spiritual vocation of the family. Its success is in direct correlation with the level of self-differentiation in the family. The deceased family member needs to be confirmed in his or her uniqueness and remembered that way. A story from the Hebrew Scriptures that stands out in this regard is the Joseph story. Father Jacob did not want to accept his son Joseph's death and refused to be comforted. Later his son did reappear, relocated in Egypt, when he fulfilled his special vocation, feeding the family of Israel in a time of famine. When Joseph dies an old man, he insists that the Israelites carry his bones with them on their ongoing journey to the Promised Land. This is a story of relocation: the dead participate in the ongoing journey of the living without becoming an obstacle on the way. The Joseph story continues in the Jesus story: a life that cannot be left behind but is carried forward into the next generation, from generation to generation.

pathological complications in the adjustment process, systemic theory locates death in the process of normal family development. While a death is often a crisis event in the life of the family, triggering disruption both in family stability and personal identity, there is also the impetus for the family to develop its resourcefulness in coping and adapting.

2. **Grief is a uniquely personal experience, not programmed by a universal, normative grief process.**
   Traditional grief theories are often classified by how they order respective predetermined stages they consider normative for the grieving process. Grief reactions that deviate from the norm are consequently deemed symptomatic, in need of corrective interventions. The systemic principle of role differentiation locates each person differently in the web of family relations, establishing uniquely personal pathways in grieving as people rework their place in the family and in life.

3. **Grief is a developmental systemic process rather a linear progression of successive stages.**
   The levels of family organization I have described as bio-physical, psychosocial and spiritual-vocational depict a multi-dimensional developmental process in the family grief experience. In the initial, acute phase of bereavement the family will often experience the loss in physical ways, with overwhelming sensations of abandonment, panic and confusion. In another phase, bereavement is felt primarily in the loss of one's place with others and the question of one's identity and place in the family and in life. In a related phase, the question of how to continue the story of the family and one's own personal journey in life takes central stage in the grieving process. Grief is not one linear process, rather, a complex configuration representing multiple, interacting levels in the psychological and developmental structure of the family.

4. **Grieving requires active personal engagement rather than submission to a predetermined healing process.**
   Attig devotes an entire chapter to the seemingly self-evident assertion that grieving is active: "Coping requires that we actively respond to what has happened to us, that we change our daily life patterns and direction in life. We must meet challenges and address tasks as we come to terms with objects, places, and events; relationships with family members, friends, fellow survivors, the deceased, and, perhaps, God; and elements of our daily routines, work and leisure lives, ongoing projects and commitments, perhaps our fundamental beliefs, and our expectations and hopes for the future" (1996, 55).
   After her husband died, Maria refused to develop another dependency, now on a therapist "prince" who would take her from the dark land of grief to the shores of new vitality and health. Instead she worked on many

levels—emotional, behavioral, relational, and cognitive—in redefining her life as an immigrant, coping with unfamiliar and stressful circumstances.

5. **Grieving is essentially a cognitive process rather than primarily an emotional experience.**
   A constructivist approach to therapy sees the task of reorienting oneself in a radically changed world as central to the grieving process. A death can fit into our life construct but can also jar our basic assumptions about life. Maria's grief left her feeling wholly displaced in the world, whether Canada or Greece.

   A person's place in the world is anchored in the emotional investments and relational bonds that sustain his or her life. That life structure and orientation schema of basic values and meanings disintegrates in a catastrophic death of a loved one, necessitating a relearning of one's world. From this constructivist perspective, emotions are "signals of the state of our meaning-making efforts," and "dimensions of transition" (Niemeyer, 1997, 172) that indicate where we are in the process of adapting to new realities and constructing new meanings.

6. **The goal of grieving is toward incorporating rather than recovering from the loss.**
   Panic and often unspeakable pain characterizes the initial, acute phase of grieving. For that reason denial often accompanies the onset of grieving, indicating the need to dull and avoid the full impact of the inner hurt. Maria wondered whether she would ever be able to look again at John's picture or mention his name without feeling that pain. In the popular mind, as well as in some grief theories and religious understandings, there is belief in an ultimate resolution or emotional recovery as the bright marker of a successful end to the grieving process. Such recovery images stem from the medical metaphor of an open wound that in time will heal and close.

   The resurrection image of the Christ figure, curiously, is a body still carrying the marks of wounds. That image may be closer to the reality of grieving. A grief resurrection does not include the disappearance of wounds. As some grief survivors have said: "You never get over the hurt but you learn to live with it." Others even fear the disappearance of their grief wound since it is one of the remaining bonds with their loved one, a mark of their caring.

7. **Grieving fosters a spiritual transformation through the relocation of the deceased.**
   Conventional grief theories, following Freud's initial bereavement model on the loss of one's love object, have emphasized the need to relinquish one's attachment to the dead and replace it with a new attachment to the living. Popular exhortations in both therapy and religion direct us in the dual, paradoxical process of accepting and letting go.

In relocation, the deceased is neither let go nor kept stuck in his or her place in the original family constellation. Rather, the person is remembered as a unique human being with a story that blends into our history and helps guide ongoing life. This approach simultaneously acknowledges the reality of the loved one's death and the ongoing awareness of the person in the life of the family and its members. Beyond the immediate goal of surviving the blow of catastrophic loss of a loved one, there is the need to incorporate the deceased in a shared history, a sacred story that carries the family forward in life. A story in the wake of trauma often requires revision of the family reality and one's personal world of meaning. The next chapter presents a narrative model that seeks to include the loss as a vital part in the ongoing story of the family and the people in it.

CHAPTER 11

Parental Loss and Marital Grief: A Case Study

THE HISTORY OF FAMILY SYSTEMS theory displays a shifting rather than fixed focus in its emphasis on what matters most in human experience, and consequently, where therapeutic intervention toward change is most useful. Family interaction sequences (time) and family system structure (space) were the initial performance domains in the practice of family therapy. The focus in the current context of social constructionism is on story which incorporates the time and space dimensions through the process of meaning-making. Narrative theory explores how human experience is shaped by meaning- making stories and proposes that we are both the creators and the creations of the stories we live by. Narrative therapy critically assesses the impact of our personal and communal stories, and through therapeutic conversation, seeks to reinterpret, sometimes rewrite, closed and oppressive stories into alternative versions which open to life and include our creative participation.

Life-and-Death Stories

In human existence life and death are constant companions. Our hopes and dreams for a full life are bracketed by the awareness of our mortality. A reality orientation places constraints on our grandiose ambitions and narcissistic strivings and locates mature judgment in that precarious balancing act between challenging and limiting ourselves. Stories mediate between life and death. Pushing the confines of finitude, a courageous story becomes a cosmic tale. Out of a Genesis context of a "formless void," the narrator constructs a script which provides cohesion and meaning, provoking our emotions and loyalties. Narrative theory sees stories as the media by which we shape our experiences and conversely are being shaped in what we experience as we navigate the life-and-death balances in our lives.

Some life-and-death stories tilt more toward life, others more to death. Life stories expand our lives by connecting us with other people, places, ideas, and projects in ways which enlarge our perspectives and expectations. Life-giving stories do not deny death but defy its dampening of the creative challenges of life. Life stories are the stories of courage; the courage Tillich defined as "self-affirmation 'in-spite-of,' that is in spite of that which tends to prevent the self from affirming itself" (1952, 32). When significant work and love relations fail we are inclined toward a *death*-reading in which the creative possibilities of our lives are overshadowed by the major themes of loss, restriction, and helplessness. From a narrative perspective, grieving our losses is to incorporate the losses in our life story and to reestablish a life-and-death balance that allows the telling and living of ongoing life. Thomas Attig (1996), in his illuminating storytelling grief study, aptly uses the metaphor "relearning the world" in describing the process of grieving.

The following story is about a couple losing a deeply loved child, their youngest daughter who had just turned 18, ready to leave home for university. Suffering a devastating blow and overwhelming sense of loss, the couple struggle for life to continue. The approach here is unusual—the couple are my wife and I, the child our daughter Martina. I narrate the passage below. In the commentary that follows I speak of our family in the third person.

We still vividly remember standing pushed against the railing, the huge ocean liner slowly moving away from shore, blowing its foreboding horn and releasing clouds of steam and diesel fumes, the turbulent waters separating us slowly but irreversibly from our family. This image tells the story of the beginnings of our marriage. At least geographically, we left home. We were young, determined, insisting on going our own way.

We had been married for all of five days when we left. Initiated into couplehood, a bit too young to the liking of our family, I at 24 barely look 20, the age of my bride, Myra. I had arranged a transfer from theological studies in Europe to a seminary in America. The date was 1961, well before the concept of long-distance commuter relationships.

In the early years of our marriage we developed a strong team relationship in which my seminary program and vocational aspirations were the goals toward which we both worked. Our first child, Paul, born in our second year, did not distract us from this primary commitment. When our daughter Trish was born two years later I was in my final year of seminary. Trish marked the transition to a new chapter in our existence: life in the parish. It was in a parish in Canada, a place where we celebrated the first fruition of our youthful ambitions, that Martina was born. As a further symbol of our ideals and vitality, the following year we adopted our last child, Steven.

After the second parish our lives appeared to revert to our first immigrant experience. I returned to school for graduate studies. This time the "new world" we moved to was California. We had been married for twelve years and now as a family we lived our immigrant myth of daring all in search of new possibilities.

Myra began pursuing her own academic program during our four years in the United States. Upon our return to Canada she completed an M.S.W. and started her professional career in social work. It was at that transitional time of increasing self-differentiation in the marital relationship and the stresses and demands of our by-then four teenage children, that our couple relationship felt most at risk. While our lives had been centered mainly around my career, we now entered a time when differences, including conflicts and resentments, punctuated and reshaped our relationship.

A major transition occurred when we were married close to twenty-five years. This anniversary is symbolized in the purchase of our first house, a century-old, dilapidated dwelling in a small village, with a magnificent view of the river and its flood lands. We sat on the old back-door steps and couldn't believe that this was ours. It represented a shift from being on the move to something new to finding our place in something old and permanent.

We were settling into a next phase where we reconnected as a couple. We were established in and content with our respective careers. We were launching our children. Paul had just got married (we think a bit young, barely 24). Trish was in college in the U.S. Our two youngest children, Martina and Steven, were finishing high school and living at home, in unfinished rooms filled with the smell of fresh paint.

Then comes a restless night. Myra can't sleep, worried about Martina who has been out for the weekend with two girlfriends and is due back this evening. When it gets close to two o'clock in the morning, both of us are frightened. We call the other parents on the phone and hear of a fatal car accident involving the three girls. Then the police call: Martina is dead.

The two of us, with Steve in the middle, huddle and scream in protest. What has happened is unspeakable and inconceivable. We, experts in novel experiences, are overwhelmed by our loss and helplessness. As a couple we cling together, bonded in grief. Whatever rules there might be about "right ways" of grieving, we don't care and indulge in our suffering. Even though we have already missed one night we both resist going to bed the next night. We simply cannot pretend that life goes on without Martina.

With Martina's death, our own lives also have reached some ending. While we used to enjoy watching the news, meeting interesting people, and going to the movies, our own life has become dominant, we don't want to hear other stories. Martina has become our boundary, setting us apart from both past and future.

While we cling together we become aware that we are separated by different styles of grieving. Myra listens, almost on a daily basis for the first year, to "Martina's music." She also repeatedly plays the recording of the funeral service. Yet, by doing this grief work mainly on her own time, Myra accepts that what is a comfort to her is an irritant to me. We learn that one of the many paradoxes of grief is that the more personal boundaries collapse, the more the other person demands respect as a separate individual.

Each of us is flooded by unique feelings of attachment to our daughter. Myra is aware how with Martina she can celebrate life, being endorsed and blessed as a parent. I become increasingly aware that Martina, even at 18, is still my "baby," a word I endlessly repeat as a mantra. With her I am drawn by feelings of tenderness, playfulness, indulgence. At this crucial time in the life cycle of a couple in the mid-years, we experience Martina's meaning in rejuvenating and validating our lives.

We know that Martina holds the power to make or break us as a couple and as a family. We look for her in her death, to find the images and words that will articulate who she is for us. We find that those who can tell us stories about Martina, who bring living memories, are most comforting to us in our grief. We strive to compensate for the physical loss by expanding the memories. More and more of our energy goes into building living images. We begin to sift through a pile of old pictures, letters, mementos, baby-book collections—trying to piece together a life, creating a canvas of reflections, a collage of impressions of one never to be forgotten.

Although I am not known around the house as a handyman, I start rebuilding Martina's unfinished room into a study, using thick, solid golden pine for book shelves, incorporating her many sport trophies, soccer boots and ski caps, posters and pictures. Myra commissions an artist who is to create a huge steel garden sculpture of three geese, spreading their wings as they head for the river. Another artist, Myra's sister, makes a bronze head depicting Martina to be placed just outside our large living room window overlooking the flood lands.

Our couple division of functions and roles continues in the patterns of grieving. Myra is the ritual coordinator: she organizes frequent get-togethers and special events, punctuating our family experience with significant remembrances and celebrations. Each year in July, on the weekend that the three girls were killed, we go early in the morning into the fields, picking wildflowers to take to the gravesites.

Three years after the accident (we keep calling it "the accident"—something that never should have happened), we invite all those who have been close to us in our loss to a memorial event. The sculpture of the three geese has been completed and placed in the garden. Relatives from Europe gather with friends and coworkers. We celebrate that life goes on and that Martina is a treasured part of that life.

This violent, destructive event of a car with three young girls hitting a truck, parked without lights at the side of the highway, tells the story of us as a couple. Unexpectedly, we, at full speed, ran into something unforgiving and unforeseen. It should have killed us. How did we survive? Naked and wounded on the side of the road, we began a new journey. And we found a bond we did not ask for, but one that we cannot, like a child, conceive of ever losing.

Conjoint Stories

Stories of parental loss usually tell of the grief of either mothers or fathers. The above story is one of couple grief. A narrative approach in family therapy emphasizes how individual stories are embedded in shared relational contexts. Each separate story is rooted in family, culture, and religion. Intensely personal stories often are the closest links with others. Personal stories focus on the self-reflective, meaning-making center of our lives. It is that focus in the human psyche which functions as one's soul: the inner narrator who addresses the life-and-death questions of who we are and what we care about in life. In intimate couple relationships two "narrators" find each other in and for a joint story: "This meshing of two distinct personal mythologies forms the basis of the couple's conjugal mythology" (Bargarozzi & Anderson, 1989).

A prominent theme in Peter and Myra's story is the emigration narrative. Their marriage starts on the ocean liner which separates them from country and family but binds them together as they move into a new world. The theme of expansion and challenge tilts the life-death balance strongly toward new life. This "conjugal myth" becomes a "family myth," directing and invigorating them as a young family into a new odyssey across a continent. In the marital life cycle, expansion is balanced by contraction, separation by attachment. When the children are leaving home, Myra and Peter move to their own home in a small village at the river's edge—a metaphor of a narrowing and deepening spectrum of time and space. It is at this crucial time of transition that Martina suddenly dies, an event that reverses the balance and thrusts the parents into a new search for their place in the world.

Parent Stories, Child Stories

How is the child a reflection of what is treasured in the couple relationship? Family systems literature is replete with case studies of children reflecting not so much marital aspirations as marital disappointments and conflicts through divisive triangle formations and abusive scapegoat scenarios.

Similarly, marital grief can be less organized by conjugal ideals than by conflicts now focused on differing and competing individual styles of grieving or by a heightened awareness of the spouse's absence as partner. The stress of the death of a child can hasten a timely or precipitate an untimely death of the marital relationship. Ample evidence has been cited that parental grief leads to an increase in marital stress and divorce (Rando, 1986).

From a narrative perspective, the child initially represents the hope and life aspirations which each partner brings to the marriage and which construct the conjugal myth. In intimate relationships a shared representation of the *ideal child*—the *inner child* of the couple—evolves as the prototype for the unsuspecting child who comes into the world. In the emotionally charged context of the conjugal myth, the child is to become the narrator of that myth in expressing, at least to some extent, parental hopes and ideals. Parental loss of a child through death is generally recognized in the literature as particularly traumatic and protracted. This is highlighted in a narrative understanding which sees the parent-child attachment energized by the power of shared mythology. The loss of a child is the loss of a relationship in which parents treasure inner meanings that transcend the limitations of time and space in their own lives, reaching beyond their past and present into a hope-charged future.

To have a child is to know, in diverse ways and to various degrees, what it is to lose a child. The story of the child Jesus getting lost, setting the stage for his parents' frantic search, is a universal story. Most children get lost; seldom are they found "in the temple, sitting among the teachers" (Luke 2:46). Children need to get lost in order to be found by their parents as unique human beings, each with their own sacred vocation in life. When children leave home, go their own way and speak their own minds, parents feel the anxiety of loss. Paradoxically, leaving home paves the way to come home and to be truly *at home* with each other. The story of the prodigal's older brother (Luke 15:11-32) illustrates that more can be lost when children stay home. When children never leave home, whether physically or emotionally, the parents are the ones who can end up feeling lost, not able to find themselves in lives that carry them forward.

The meaning of the loss of a child in Myra and Peter's story is expressed through the leaving home metaphor. When a child successfully leaves home, coming home becomes possible, and parents and children can meet as adults who freely come and go without getting lost. When a child dies before having left home, the death aborts the leaving home transition, leaving parents stuck in their parental vocation. When a child dies after having successfully left home, the death aborts the coming home event, leaving parents stuck with a life robbed from a future. Peter and Myra grieve the death of their child who is at the crucial point of leaving home, ready to live a life. Their grief is saturated with the sadness of profound parental deprivation and the anger about the incredible waste of life.

Spiritual Perspectives

Charles Gerkin has expanded Anton Boisen's image of "the living human document" from a hermeneutical perspective, stating that "Boisen was fundamentally correct in his placing of the crux of human suffering at the point of the connection between experience and idea, between the occurrence of events and a language of meaning for those events. It is when that connection becomes blocked, distorted, or made impossible that the troubled person must seek a helper, an interpreter who may offer a new possibility of meaning" (1989, 53).

Narrative care attends to the stories of suffering by focusing on signals of the courage to live. In a hermeneutical context of spiritual care our stories are heard as private but not isolated stories, reflected upon and interpreted in connection with other stories and other languages of meaning. The metaphors of spirituality hold out bridges to traditions and communities of faith committed to courageous living.

Marital grief counseling primarily focuses on the conjugal myth, where life dynamics stand out in spite of evidence that both health and pathology, life and death, are interwoven in the process of couple formation. The narrative that typically joins two separate lives carries yearnings for reconciliation, restoration, and resolution. Spiritual care with couples attends to the "courage to be" edge in the marital narrative. Myra and Peter's conjugal myth is rooted in the emigration experience of leaving home and establishing a home on foreign soil. This narrative has the potential to organize their parental loss experience. Rather than a story of limitation it is the story of expansion which connects them to the courage to face the unknown to find a new place in the world. Scriptural referent points for theological reflection abound in the migration themes of the stories of Abraham, the wanderings of the Israelites through the wilderness, and the death-and-resurrection transformations in Jesus's ministry. The life-and-death balance is especially significant in the process of grieving the loss of life. A preponderance of death in that balance can promote current cultural throw-away attitudes insisting on quickly replacing death separations with new life attachments. However, grief teaches that life is to be found in rather than *apart from* the losses. The story of Myra and Peter illustrates a stubborn refusal to let go of their child but "to piece together a life, creating a canvas of images, a collage of impressions of one never to be forgotten." A grief that actively works with the loss of life resists replacement and searches for a process of relocation of the loved one in an enduring and transforming presence which empowers ongoing life.

Narrative theory initially appears to represent primarily a cognitive and individualistic approach, emphasizing the uniquely personal ways in which the mind organizes experience and authors the meanings of life. The "conjugal myth" illustrates that our narratives are also relational, social and behavioral, like plays which recruit actors who rehearse their individual lines for joint, public performances. Narratives are produced in social interaction, welding word and action the way that the Hebrew Scriptures use one word to denote both meanings. Grieving is the process of addressing losses that have radically disturbed and, against our will, rewritten the stories we live by. Myra and Peter initially dwell in their grief, in the defiance of "we don't care and we indulge in our suffering," symbolized in not going to bed to wake up in a new day, refusing to leave the old world for a new world without Martina. Grieving becomes grief work when we go beyond our losses by redefining ourselves in our many relationships and by reenacting our place in the world.

Pastoral care is expressed in the public ministry of word and ritual; it facilitates life's common transitions and marks the endings and beginnings in our lives. The story of Myra and Peter illustrates need to create additional particular spiritual rituals. As a couple, long-time students of the liturgical pedagogy of their religious community, they write ritual scripts to punctuate and process the changes in their life. There are the rituals of remembering: a memory book, garden sculptures symbolizing an ongoing presence, anniversary days of gathering wildflowers and meeting at the grave sites. There are rituals of endings and of beginning: the transformation of Martina's room into a study and workplace, the memorial celebration marking reentry into life with friends and relatives.

In listening to the conjugal myth, the therapist hears the multi-layered stories which constitute the couple's texture of life, a texture now torn in grief. Parental loss disrupts the natural order of life and death; it is experienced as a jarring loss in meaning. Parental loss also violates the marital myth of producing the "ideal child" and protecting this child against all harm. After Martina's sudden and violent death, Peter and Myra identify with the accident, feeling left to die at "the side of the road." What has happened does not fit the conjugal myth. The loss of a child challenges faith in the image of God as a strong and caring parent. In marital grief comfort may not be possible without a radical theological revision. The process of "relearning the world" is a theological task in which spiritual care is challenged to facilitate new understandings in situations that defy traditional piety and rational explanation.

Summary

This chapter has described the *conjugal myth*, and its core metaphor of the *ideal child*, as the blending of what is most personal and vital in each partner's individual story. A narrative approach in parental grief ministry will focus on the conjugal myth as a source both of the suffering and for the healing. The ideal child symbolizes foremost parental life vocations and aspirations. Consequently, losing a child is the necessary condition for a child to differentiate and leave home. The loss of a child through death is the violent separation between *leaving home* and *coming home*. The challenge in parental grief ministry is to be part of preparing a home-coming for the lost child. Such a redemptive grieving process is filled with mystery and surprises. The case study in this chapter demonstrates that parental grief cannot be controlled or managed by expert outside interventions. Yet, the ministry of presence offers more than company when it actively participates in the grief work. In parental loss such work is identified in a ritual process of remembering the child, narrative scripting in which the lost child is found for an enduring presence, and the rehearsals and reenactments of a revitalized conjugal myth for ongoing life.

PART FOUR

The Study
of
Spiritual
Care

CHAPTER 12

Supervision in Learning and Teaching Spiritual Care

MY FIRST EXPERIENCE OF SUPERVISION took place in a clinical pastoral education program. I began in a state of awe inspired by the stature of the chaplain supervisor. He seemed comfortable in the hospital, a place that intimidated me. He moved with apparent ease and confidence in a world of human frailty and suffering, surrounded by busy nurses, authoritative doctors and the complex administrative structures of a large bureaucratic system. In the course of the term, the program's focus seemed to shift to me as the student. I became increasingly aware of my own blocks and growing edges as I critically reflected on my clinical experience. Some of us students felt that rather than more skills we needed therapy. All of us learned that in order to give care we require much care ourselves. Years later, when I prepared my "model of supervision" in applying to become a supervisor myself, I reflected on these early experiences:

> The genius of Supervised Pastoral Education (SPE) is in its complexity as a multi-dimensional process of education. SPE takes place within an intricate network of interrelationships which focuses on the self, others, and encounters between the self and others in a variety of helping contexts. When SPE ceases to be such a complex process, it can become abusive. A simplistic view and practice of SPE tends to absolutize one or another aspect of the SPE learning process. Two extreme examples can be cited. A preoccupation with the supervisor as "guru" reduces SPE to a quasi-religious enterprise in which disciples are cultivated, while a preoccupation with the student as "patient" reduces SPE to a quasi-therapeutic enterprise in which the student's actual or potential pathology is diagnosed and, hopefully, treated. (VanKatwyk, 1988, 319-327)

A Systems Model of Supervision

In an effort to combine complexity with comprehensibility, this chapter explores the supervisory process through a systems conceptualization. Systems supervision is not the supervision of systems therapy such as family therapy. Rather, supervision itself is a multi-dimensional process composed of diverse parts—parts that in theory can be examined independently but in actual practice merge in a dynamic and intricate systemic interaction.

Supervision assists students to make meanings and develop skills from their clinical experience. At the core of supervision is the *experiential learning cycle*, which has been conceptualized as a four-phase cyclical process: *being with* others in a clinical experience and then *examining, evaluating,* and *acting upon* this experience.

This process constantly generates new clinical experiences to examine, evaluate, and act upon. There is no rigid order—the learner can start at any point in the cycle and pass through each phase from different directions and in different frequencies in the course of a cycle or round of learning. Students bring their own unique learning styles that organize these "four seasons" into personalized climates in which optimum professional and personal growth can take place (Kolb & McCarthy, 1980; O'Connor, 1994, 50-62).

While there is no clockwork precision and sequence to pacing the four phases in experiential learning, there is inner harmony. A balance arises from movement back and forth between concrete experience (being with) and abstract conceptualizing (evaluating), and between reflective observation (examining) and active experimentation (acting) (Maclean Batts & Mandsley, 1981). The various tools of clinical education, including audio/video tape recordings, supervisory feedback, written reflection reports, peer group interaction, role play, learning contracts and evaluations, are designed to engage the student in the various stages of the experiential learning cycle.

Figure 12.1 The Experiential Learning Cycle

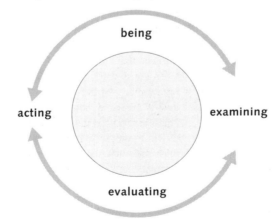

The experiential *learning cycle* is at the center of a fourfold *learning focus* consisting of the student, the client, the relationship and the larger context or environment in which that relationship takes place and is assigned a specific meaning. Shifts in learning focus are illustrated in the history of clinical pastoral education (CPE) in America. This movement started with an emphasis on neither the supervisor, nor the student but on the patient as the *living human document* (Boisen's term; see Powell, 1975). Starting in the early 1920s, Anton Boisen emphasized the significance of *case records* and *case analyses* as primary tools for understanding the patient, and in the context of the psychiatric hospital, learning about the religious meanings of mental illness. Beginning in the 1930s, the focus shifted from the patient to the student, specifically under the influence of the Russell L. Dicks with the emergence of the *conversation process record*, later refined to the *verbatim* (see Appendix 7). The one-time Boisen student Seward Hiltner became instrumental in establishing Carl Rogers's client-centered approach in pastoral care and counseling. This was not a return to Boisen's patient-centered focus toward insight, but rather embraces the more complicated relational context of student, client and the encounter between the two. By the 1960s the focus in CPE had shifted from *intra*-personal dynamics (whether the patient or student) to the *inter*-personal dynamics of *being with* others. Thus the helping relationship came into prominence as the main focus for spiritual care.

The *experiential learning focus* diagram sketches an overview of the major dimensions of supervision. While we can distinguish the four learning focus areas, in practice they interact and define themselves as one integrated system. The value of looking separately at each focus is that each highlights certain supervisory issues and processes operative in the four focus areas:

1. **The Student**

   The student brings his or her cultural identity, including gender, ethnic, socioeconomic and religious background, values and beliefs, sexual orientation, and social history. This is a person shaped by family history, theoretical orientation, level of personal awareness, and clinical readiness. These are all critical components of supervision; factors the supervisor needs to know and incorporate in the supervision. However, a singular focus on the student unavoidably shifts supervision into therapy. Since the use of self is a primary therapeutic tool in most counseling models, it is often impossible to maintain a clear boundary between supervision and therapy. Rather than simply excluding the person of the student, supervision can best include the student by focusing on the relationship roles in which the student represents himself or herself in the counseling and supervisory context. That approach will be further discussed in the section on helping styles.

2. **The Client**

   The client brings the supervisor and the student together, while the client's presenting problem organizes the supervisory agenda and frames the case conceptualization (see chapter 4). The client can be one person or a relationship that presents itself for therapy. The supervisor normally hears about the client's presenting problem from the student. In supervision, then, the presenting problem presents both client and student. The supervisor can choose where to place himself or herself on the continuum between the client and the student. As a representative of the client's best interests, the supervisor uses supervision to direct the therapy through the student. As a representative of the student's best interests, the supervisor uses supervision to educate the student through the client. Rather than a linear continuum of polar opposites, in reality supervision may resemble more of a triangle where the supervisor constantly balances the interests of both client and student.

3. **The Relationship**
   The relationship focuses on how the student presents himself or herself in the various contexts as counselor, student, staff member, peer and colleague. Such social roles indicate how the person participates in the various systems. Following the historical migration of the point of focus in the clinical pastoral education movement—from patient to student to their relationship—this chapter, following Part 2, centers on the relationship. (Helping Styles, below, explores the various helping postures between counselor and client, and, in parallel fashion, between supervisor and student.)

4. **The Context**
   The supervisor functions in the larger context of a health care organization and professional, educational and religious communities with their respective guiding structures of rules and regulations. Sometimes the primary context of supervision is administrative and managerial in nature.

Figure 12.2   The Experiential Learning Focus

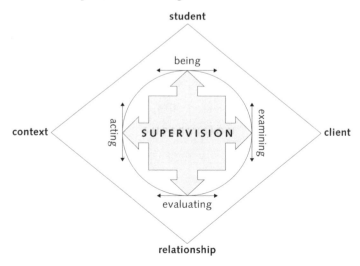

In clinical supervision the focus is primarily educational. The educational context includes the learning contract with the evaluation process reflecting goals and expectations, theological reflection on the clinical experience, theoretical exploration and innovative practice experimentation. The professional and religious context includes standards of practice, professional codes of ethics (see Appendixes 9 & 10), and religious practices and beliefs from an inclusive, cross-cultural perspective.

Helping Styles

The supervisor's vision and understanding of the goal of supervision vitalizes and directs the process. The goal of supervision pursued in this chapter is found in the triad of what to know, what to do and what to be (see chapter 7). The goal of supervision is to connect what to know (theory) and what to do (practice) in what to be (the helping relationship). The crucial bridge between theory and practice is the therapist's use of self in the act of caring. It seems ironical that what is most at the core of supervision often is least accessible. My supervision experience has shown that students, at least initially, prefer supervision to focus on the client. There is a reluctance to move from the client and the presenting problem to the immediacy of the helping relationship and of what is going on in the therapy room. Simple supervisory questions like, "What do you like/dislike most about this client?" or "How do you imagine the client sees you?" can be disorienting because of the shift of focus from the client to the student and the helping relationship.

The master practitioner/teacher Salvador Minuchin asks, "What kind of therapist do I aim to co-create in supervision?" (1997, 278). His answer brings together the therapist's knowledge and techniques for use of self: "This therapist has an hypothesis about the best way to help this family. She knows that any hypothesis is only tentative, a map to be changed whenever new information makes a better fit possible. That means a therapist who can take possession of many partial truths and use them as probes, until the family responds and a better fit can be calibrated. She needs to know herself sufficiently well to access the parts of herself that are useful for the therapeutic goal. She needs to have a map of final goals, along with the ability to zigzag in whatever way the process requires, while keeping the goals in mind" (278).

From this perspective, supervision begins with the student's habitual and routine ways of being helpful or doing therapy. Minuchin uses the term "the therapist's style" to describe this focus of supervision: "To reach the goal of a therapist who is both strategic and self-aware, I have learned in my supervision to focus on the therapist's style—that is, on his or her use of a preferred, narrow set of predictable responses under a variety of diverse circumstances." The goal of supervision is first to ascertain the student's therapeutic style and then go beyond it: "What are the responses in their repertory that they utilize most frequently? We accept them. They are okay. Then we declare them wanting. The therapist's style is all right as far as it goes, but it can be enlarged" (1997, 278).

The *Helping Style Inventory* (HSI; the core conceptualization of Part 2 and described in detail in chapter 7) maps the major helping styles and images. Designed to span the scope and classify the diversity of helping styles, as a tool of supervision it draws the profile of the student's distinctive or dominant helping style. The purpose is not to invalidate this helping style profile, even though it may have only limited therapeutic applications, but to encourage students to extend themselves into new territory.

Figure 12.3   The Helping Style Inventory

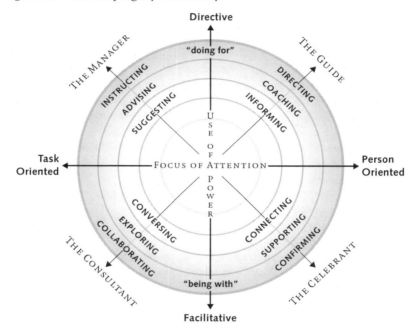

The HSI approach fits the experiential learning cycle: students get specific feedback with which to examine, evaluate, expand and modify their caring responses. The feedback is not primarily confrontational or evaluative but part of an adult learning process activated by tape-recorded, verbatim-reported counseling excerpts or actual clinical experiences or role-plays that are shared and examined in a collaborative context. The HSI avoids the defensive preoccupation of students with questions of right and wrong, and fosters the supervision hypothesis that regular and primarily descriptive feedback works well in the experiential learning cycle.

The Supervisory Relationship

In supervision, the supervisory relationship itself is the most potent case in point of a differential use of *helping styles*. As depicted in Figure 12.2, the supervisory relationship is at the center of students' experiential learning process. The supervisor brings his or her own personal history, values, cultural identity, and theoretical orientation into a professionally defined working relationship with students. The quality of the supervisory relationship hinges on how the supervisory roles and tasks are integrated with a personal, mutual involvement between supervisor and student.

Holloway (1995) distinguishes between the functions and tasks of supervision. The *tasks* are content areas of basic competencies expected from the student, such as counseling skills, case conceptualization and professional identity. The supervision *functions* are process oriented: monitoring/evaluating, advising/instructing, modeling, consulting, and supporting/sharing. These process functions are represented in the HSI as helping behaviors that define particular helping images: manager, guide, consultant, and celebrant. Williams's (1995) model of supervision integrates four supervisory roles with six supervision focus areas into a *role-focus matrix*. The supervisory roles (teacher, facilitator, consultant, evaluator) parallel the respective HSI helping images of guide, celebrant, consultant, and manager. Williams's *six-focus approach* correlates the therapy system with the supervisory system, resembling the *experiential learning focus* framework (Figure 12.2) described in this chapter.

The respective frameworks of Holloway and Williams are examples of a systems approach to supervision emphasizing the multi-dimensional nature and the relational core of supervision. The *Helping Style Inventory* combines diversity with a single focus on the helping relationship. Interpersonal patterns connect the therapy system and the supervisory system. In doing supervision, I often become aware how the supervisory system and the therapy system mirror each other. When the supervisor focuses on the joining between therapist and client (the therapy system), the joining between supervisor and student (the supervisory system) becomes the mirror. When the student presents a client who "talks too much and will not listen," the "talk and listen" interaction between student and supervisor becomes the mirror. In teaching diversity in helping, the supervisor's own flexible and playful use of different parts of the self becomes the mirror.

Of special significance—and concern—is the *use of power* in supervision. In view of the nature of supervisory tasks and roles, the relationship is unequal due to the power differential between the supervisor and the student. In the context of the HSI model, the vertical "use of power" continuum stretches from the *directive* end (power localized in the supervisor) to the *facilitative* end (power localized in the student). The ideal is not to polarize but to balance these two ends on the power continuum. In a balanced supervisory relationship both power and empowerment are present, each including the other. Directiveness and facilitation are not mutually exclusive helping styles but function codependently. In supervision, power does not reside exclusively in either the supervisor or the student, but comes to play in their mutual involvement in the supervisory relationship.

The same applies to the horizontal *focus of attention* HSI continuum stretching from the *task*—to the *person*-orientation. In the history of therapy, this continuum has been frequently subject to polarization where one end is favored over the other (see chapter 7 for a discussion of these opposites in a therapy context). A more flexible supervisory style is evident when the tasks of supervision are balanced with the needs of the person. At times most of the attention can focus on the task, balanced by other times when the attention shifts to the person as affected by the task.

The polarization of the two HSI continuums is often presented as gender specific: male helping/supervising as typically task-focused and directive in contrast with a female approach that is typically affiliative, self-disclosing, and non-directive. While encouraging differences in individual supervision styles, the HSI resists gender or any other polarization in favor of the ideal of an inclusive, contextual approach that claims the whole map. Yet it is evident that power and gender are not disconnected but bound in cultural, historical, and systemic ties. Research studies show that clinical supervision has often been experienced as male-dominated and hierarchical, especially when few women supervisors represent the professional association.[1] In a study of women's experience of pastoral supervision in the *Canadian Association of Pastoral Practice and Education*, Elizabeth Meakes and Tom O'Connor, report: "Generally, the data showed that female supervisees were empowered by a supervision approach which respected the uniqueness of females' experiences in ministry, built on the learning style of the supervisee, and used a learning contract and a more collaborative supervision style" (1993, p. 36). In view of the inherent potential for the abuse of power and insensitivity to women's experiences, I support the suggestion to use dyadic supervision where students have more presence and can more readily adopt the role of consultants and contributors in the supervisory process.

The developmental nature of supervision is another significant feature of supervisory relationships. These relationships are not static but in constant flux as they evolve over time. A developmental perspective tracks the stages through which supervision moves: from the initial stage of establishing a working relationship, to a real relationship that is less role bound and more interpersonal, to the terminating stage when the goals of supervision have been realized and the supervisory relationship is being replaced with a peer relationship. Holloway highlights the "mature phase" when the supervisory relationship

---

1   Thomas St James O'Connor (1998) observes that in 1990 50 percent of the membership of the *Canadian Association for Pastoral Practice and Education* (CAPPE) was made up of women but only 10 percent of the membership represented full teaching supervisors.

becomes more interpersonal: "After initial interactions, participants come to know one another better and are thus more accurate in their messages. With decreased uncertainty, they are better able to use control strategies and communicative modes that will reduce the level of conflict in the relationship. Participants also become increasingly more vulnerable and more willing to risk self-disclosure, whereas in the initial stages, genuine self-disclosure is seldom observed" (1995, 49). This description sees the development of the supervisory relationship as analogous to the therapy relationship in its focus on building a secure interpersonal climate with a more open and less defensive style of communication.

Another developmental perspective (Stoltenberg & Delworth, 1987) focuses not so much on the supervisory relationship as on the student's learning level. Here the emphasis is on matching the style of supervision with the level of the student's development as a counselor. The HSI Map can be used to track such shifts in supervisory style. The developmental approach assumes that at a basic level, students are best served by supervisors who provide both guidance and structure. According to the HSI Map, the appropriate supervision style for this level of training is predominantly *directively person-oriented*, combining direction and support. However, a next phase in supervision may well be a shift to a *facilitatively person-directed style*, allowing the supervisor to become less directive and more supportive, confirming, and celebrating the student's budding efforts in counseling. When students reach a more advanced level, however, the assumption is that there is less need for personal support and encouragement— although who can do without it?—but more need for a practice-focus in supervision. This developmental process is expressed in a shift to a *facilitatively task-oriented* style that defines supervision as primarily a collaborative and consultative process.

A Supervision Case Illustration

The following is a composite picture taken from my supervision experience in an interdisciplinary setting. David is a student in a combined masters degree program in theology and social work and has his first clinical placement in a pastoral counseling center. The supervisor has done the assessment interview of a client, Mrs Clare, who is assigned to David. David has read the following information from the assessment report before the interview.

Mrs Clare became a widow with the sudden death of her husband three months ago. Her daughter separated from her husband about the same time. She and her two young children came to live with Mrs Clare, and soon conflict erupted between the two women. Mrs Clare has come to the counseling center to present the mounting tension with her daughter, but has refused the recommendation of the assessment counselor for joint therapy with her daughter to address the relational conflict.

David made an audio tape of the first session and had selected the following short excerpt for supervision:

(C = Client, Mrs Clare; D = Counselor, David)

C.1   I have already told the other counselor [during the assessment] about my daughter. I am glad that you will be the counselor because you seem more open-minded and are closer to her age, you might be better able to talk with her.

D.1   You have concerns about your daughter. And I understand she lives with you now.

C.2   Yes, she came to live with me the month after my husband died. She has the two children too. She separated from her husband who is abusive. His personality changed the day after the marriage. All of this has changed her personality too. She used to be so easy to get along with, but now she is impossible.

D.2   There have been a lot of changes for you—your husband's death and then within a few weeks your daughter's separation....

C.3   (a long silence followed by the sound of crying)

D.3   No time for yourself. So busy having to think of others....

C.4   (long silence with more sobbing)

D.4   Can you tell me a bit more about your daughter, Mrs Clare?

C.5   (After a pause)... She really wanted her husband to come back but he refused. He is already with somebody else. I don't understand why she has to be so miserable. She is better without him.

D.5   It sounds to me that she is grieving for her husband and the loss of her marriage.

C.6   I think she needs psychiatric help. But she doesn't want help. She doesn't think she needs it. She refuses when I mention it to her. I can't take any more. (deep sigh)

D.6   You have already taken a lot. I can understand it feels like getting too much.

C.7   I was thinking that I can ask my daughter to take me for the next appointment and that you invite her in and talk to her.

D.7   I can do that but I would appreciate if you tell her that I'd like to talk to both of you.

C.8   If I do, she will not come with me. I know it.

D.8   Well...okay...let's see what happens.

Tracking David's responses on the HSI diagram, presents the following profile of his helping style:

Figure 12.4   Student Helping Style Profile

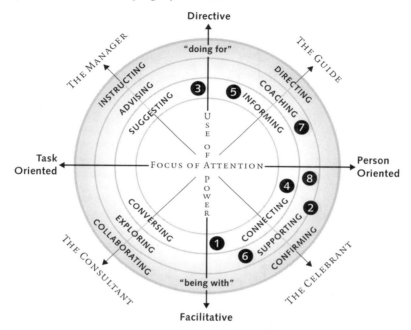

David's dominant helping stance in this short interaction with Mrs Clare is *person-oriented* and, appropriately for a first interview, the *facilitative* end stands out in connecting and supporting responses. At times David becomes more directive: once in presenting a challenge and suggestion (D.3), and twice in offering new information or guidance (D.5 & 7). The HSI profile is positive for a beginning therapist in showing some movement on the map through helping behaviors of a low rather than extreme level of intensity. In a global and provisional assessment based on the above HSI profile, the following features of David's therapeutic style can be noted at this point:

- David presents himself in a respectful, non-threatening and polite fashion. Beyond merely joining, David reaches out in empathy (D.2), trying to understand and connect with the client's pain.

- David is sensitive to the client's feelings to the point of accommodating (D.8).

- This sensitivity can lead to rescuing attempts. In D.4 David seems to rescue Mrs Clare from the long silence and the sobbing. In D.5 David appears to rescue the daughter from her mother's attacks. It suggests that David tends to get pulled into an advocacy role or compassionate counseling model whenever a person is suffering or is being put down.

- This concern for others seems to override David's ability to speak up for himself or own his perceptions. In D.3 he turns away from pursuing the grief as a counseling issue when the client seems to resist that path. Even though he expresses his own opinion in D.7, he readily, though unhappily, surrenders to the client's point of view in D.8: "Well ... okay ...."

The HSI profile draws a global and generalized picture of the student's relational style in contrast to the fourfold *learning focus* that explores more distinct though related issues. The following section probing the four focus areas in the case of Mrs Clare and her daughter provides a wider supervisory scope:

1. **The Student**
   When the supervisor asked David what he liked most about Mrs Clare, he responded that he felt drawn to her because she was struggling courageously under stressful circumstances. David had more difficulty in expressing what he disliked about his client. When the supervisor pushed the issue, David became more aware that he was "uncomfortable" with her "demanding attitude" and that he felt "pushed" by her into something he did not like to do (D.8). When the supervisor asked how David imagined Mrs Clare perceived him, David, after some more supervisory prodding, responded that he felt that she saw him as her son. Following this family transference, David shared that he experiences angry feelings with his own mother, a widow quite dependent on him as the only child but who at the same time seems impossible to please. In recounting this family scenario, David has shared a troubled agenda that invites personal therapy. To stay within the bounds of supervision, the supervisor focused on the supervisory relationship, asking parallel process questions: "How did it feel when I pushed you to answer some tough questions?" and "How would it be for you to try out different, less polite, responses to being pushed and prodded, and do so in the safety of the learning setting of our supervision time?"

2. **The Client**
   There is disagreement about "who is the client?" in the case of Mrs Clare. The assessment counselor proposed that she come in with her daughter, presenting their relationship as the client. Instead, Mrs Clare presents the daughter as the identified client and recruits David as her daughter's counselor. In the absence of the daughter, David is prepared to do the counseling with Mrs Clare as the client. These three variant client identifications need to be evaluated in supervision. Strategies of how to invite the daughter to participate with her mother in counseling can be discussed. *The mother-*

daughter relationship as client can be conceptualized as two women mutually grieving marital loss and displacing the pain on each other. This perspective offers another option: to separate Mrs Clare and her daughter through a structural approach of seeing each woman individually in counseling, if each consents to such a parallel arrangement, preferably with two different counselors. At this initial juncture, supervision will focus on the need to clarify the counseling contract, knowing that Mrs Clare's plan of being the adjunct in the counseling of her daughter will duplicate the family problem and effectively sabotage all therapeutic possibilities.

3. **The Relationship**
   In the first focus area on the student, David's personal issues with his mother were addressed in the supervisory context: how David responds to demands made of him, especially when these are in conflict with his own ideas and values. This approach focuses on therapeutic helping styles and emphasizes that David's present style of accommodating only serves to reinforce rather than challenge symptomatic client demand behavior. The supervisor situated these therapy issues in the supervision, importing "pushy" and "demanding" behaviors through her use of self. A supervisory task will be to coach David in alternative styles of therapeutic responses (see chapter 4) with an emphasis on I-messages which, with the exception of D.7, are missing in the recorded segment.

4. **The Context**
   The short interaction with Mrs Clare raises several contextual issues including:

   - The ethical nature of conspiring with Mrs Clare to get the daughter into counseling. The counselor's forming an alliance with the client in targeting the daughter as the identified problem creates a triangle which compromises therapy for both the mother and the daughter. The duplicity of luring the daughter into counseling is a breach of the principle of "informed consent" as expressed in the various professional codes of ethics.

   - The larger therapeutic question of what constitutes help as a focus for theological reflection. When is help unhelpful? What is the therapeutic value of saying no? How does rebuff fit our philosophy of caring and, more specifically, our own helping image?

   - The agency's practice of splitting the assessment interview from the subsequent counseling relationship. In this case, the supervisor has a dual relationship as the initial assessment counselor and as supervisor of the assigned counselor, potentially contaminating the ongoing supervisory relationship. Mrs C's opening line to David in the recorded excerpt— C.1: "I am glad that you will be the counselor…"—appears to be an attempt at triangulating the student, with the potential of bringing the therapy system in competition with the supervisory system. Mrs Clare favors David over the supervisor (as the assessment counselor) for being more open and accessible. In choosing this segment for supervision, is David sending a message for his supervisor to back off?

Summary

The above discussion of the fourfold *experiential learning focus* is far from exhaustive but illustrates how each focus area raises its own specific supervisory issues. The objective of the chapter is to connect the various supervisory tasks and functions in a comprehensive *systems model* of supervision. In line with the tradition of spiritual care, the heart of supervision is the supervisory relationship. The *Helping Style Inventory* model defines the helping relationship in therapy and supervision as filled with diversity. The HSI promotes the goal of supervision toward a creative, informed, and daring use of self in the practice of caring. The *experiential learning cycle* respects the personal integrity and unique style of each student, and challenges the same student to experience novelty and intimacy in learning through *living human documents*.

CHAPTER 13

Research Methods in Spirituality and Health Care
—*Thomas St James O'Connor*

PERSONS INVOLVED IN SPIRITUAL CARE often find the word "research" challenging. Many think that research involves large samples, statistical analysis and incomprehensible language and concepts. Some are suspicious of research, believing that it serves the interests of the researchers and/or funders. Others wonder if research has any significance for clinical work. There is little empirical research in the pastoral care and counseling literature (Gartner et al., 1990; VandeCreek, 1995; O'Connor et al., 2001b). This chapter examines a series of questions: What is research? What are various research methods? How can the evidence from research be used in clinical work? What is evidence-based clinical work? In answering these questions, concrete examples from the research are provided. The chapter also describes several research methods to be critiqued, celebrated, and implemented in the pastoral and clinical area. A clinical approach incorporating evidence from the research is endorsed.

Research in Spiritual Care

Social scientist Bruce Berg says that "the purpose of research is to discover answers to questions through the application of systematic procedures" (1997, 7). Pastoral supervisor and academic Anne Sutherland says that "research is an orderly and rational way to explore and seek answers to questions" (1995, 2). Douglas Sprenkle and Sidney Moon, family therapists, and researchers, describe research as a variety of "strategies or procedures that can be utilized to answer research questions" (1996a, 8). Research, then, requires a question(s) to which the researcher seeks an answer(s). There are many examples of research questions:

- Does a *solution-focused first formula* session task (FFST) clarify treatment goals, create compliance, and produce a positive outcome in therapy? (Adams et al., 1991)
- Is religion good for your health? (Koenig, 1997)

- What are the effects of hospital chaplains on the health of their patients? (VandeCreek, 1994)
- What are clients' experiences of narrative therapy? (O'Connor, Meakes, et al., 1997b)
- What is authentic helping in pastoral ministry? (VanKatwyk, 1988, 1995)
- Does pastoral counseling belong in the congregation? (O'Connor, 1999)

Every clinician develops questions from the practice of ministry. The challenge is to develop the questions into a refined research question that can be answered.

Developing a viable research question is not always easy. Most researchers take some time to refine the question, often through conversation with other clinicians and researchers, reading, reflection, and much hard work. Larry VandeCreek notes two obstacles to refining the question: refusal to engage in the refining and clarification process, and formulating the question too soon. The initial research query can contain many questions. VandeCreek gives an example of the struggle of formulating a question (1994, 34-41), His question is "What are the effects of hospital chaplains on patients?" He writes down the question and then begins to play with the words in the question. He critiques each verb, noun and adjective until he finds the wording that is appropriate and fits for what he wants to know.

Systematic Procedures

Systematic procedures involve the methods used in answering the question. Methods and systematic procedures imply a number of assumptions. First, intuition is not a systematic procedure. Intuition does play a role in the research process. The researcher often has some indications of an answer to the question before the systematic procedures even begin. The preliminary answers are most often based on intuition arising from the researcher's previous experience around the issues in the question. However, research involves clearly outlined systematic pursuit that can be replicated by another research. Second, systematic procedures seek a truthful answer. Research is the pursuit of truth. One's ability to find a truthful answer has many limits. Nevertheless, the search is essential for the research procedure. A researcher must be open to the possibility that the answer(s) to the research question(s) can be different from the researcher's initial intuition or hunches. A randomized control study that shows that a particular intervention has little or no effect is just as truthful as one that shows it has significant effect. Limitations to the discovery of a truthful answer include researcher bias, inappropriate method(s) used to pursue the question, inadequate tools to accumulate and analyze the data, a flawed interpretive process and the limitations of the context.

Larry VandeCreek, Hilary Bender, and Merle R. Jordan (1994) outline two basic research methods: quantitative and qualitative. Most texts in the social sciences follow these two methods. However, pastoral care and counseling, uses a third method: hermeneutical. These different approaches in research can be distinguished from each other as described in the following main sections of the chapter.

Quantitative Research Methods

Quantitative methods are not the most dominant systematic procedures in the field of pastoral ministry. Within the discipline of theology, Larry VandeCreek (1994, 1995b) has utilized quantitative methods in spiritual care. Outside theology, clinical epidemiologists such as Harold Koenig (1997), David Larson and Jeffrey Levin have used quantitative methods to examine the role of spirituality and religion in health. This quantitative research utilizes various methods. Randomized control trials are a classic form of research (Jadad, 1998). In a randomized control trial, usually one intervention that the researcher believes makes a difference is isolated (the independent variable). Two groups are randomly selected. A test is given to both groups at the beginning. This test or measurement is the area that the independent variable ought to impact. One group is not given the independent variable (control group), the other is (experimental group). After the independent variable has been inserted into the experimental group, the two groups are given the measurement test again. If the independent variable has had an effect, then this should show up in the difference in measurements between the experimental group and the control group.

▓ A Case Example from Spiritual Care

A randomized control study is found in the research on "Positive Therapeutic Effects of Intercessory Prayer in a Coronary Care Unit" (Bryd, 1988). Bryd believed that intercessory prayer had a positive effect on the physical health of coronary care patients. His independent variable was intercessory prayer. He selected two large groups of coronary care patients who went through the same unit. These groups were randomized and neither patients nor staff knew to which group each belonged. The experimental group had born-again Christians outside the hospital praying for their recovery. The control group did not have this. Patients in both groups were given standard tests for coronary care at the beginning of their stay in the unit. They were also given standard tests at the end. In this study, the experimental group had better health outcomes in some areas.

This randomized control trial has many strengths. There is the size of the random sample—393 patients. The study was double blind, so that neither patients nor staff could consciously affect the results. The patients all experienced the same coronary care unit so that there was not a difference in treatment. And W.S. Harris and colleagues replicated the study (Harris et al., 1999). The study also had weaknesses. First, it is impossible to completely isolate the independent variable to the experimental group. Patients in the control group who were not scheduled to experience intercessory prayer might have had relatives and friends praying for them. They would have been receiving the independent variable as well. Also this study has never been repeated by other researchers. Repeatability guards against chance results.

In quantitative research, the research question is often not present. However, a thesis or answer to the question has been developed and broken into a number of hypotheses. The goal of the research is to prove or disprove the thesis or hypothesis. Hallmarks of quantitative research are large samples and statistical representations of the data. Survey research can also be quantitative and there are many examples of it in spiritual care (O'Connor et al., 2001a). The researchers also attempt to be removed from any interaction with the participants in the study so that researcher bias will not influence the results. A randomized sample is another strategy to avoid researcher bias.

A Case Example from Family Therapy

Jerome Adams, Fred Piercy, and Joan Jurich utilized three groups in their study, "Effects of Solution Focused Therapy's 'Formula First Session Task' on Compliance and Outcome in Family Therapy" (1991). The researchers randomized clients to one control group and two experimental groups. The independent variable is the formula first session task (FFST) developed by Steve de Shazer for solution-focused therapy. The researchers wanted to see if the FFST had a positive effect on goal clarity, client compliance and treatment outcome in the improvement of the presenting problem (the dependent variables). The first experimental group received the FFST in the first session and then in sessions 2-10 followed a solution-focused approach outlined by de Shazer. The second experimental group received the FFST in the first session and then followed a structural approach to treatment in sessions 2-10. The control group followed a structural approach to treatment throughout all ten sessions. Measurements were conducted by outside observers, the families themselves and the therapists. The research found that the ffst was helpful in the initial stages on "gaining family compliance, increasing clarity of treatment goals and initiating improvement of the presenting problem" (Adams, et al., 288-289). However, it did not increase family optimism and the effects of the FFST faded by the last session. The strengths of this research include using two experimental groups and one control group. The agreement among the various raters included the observers, the therapist, and families on the effectiveness of the therapy. The weaknesses include researcher bias towards the structural family therapy at Purdue and a concern about the training of the solution-focused therapists.

Much quantitative research in spiritual care is produced by those outside theological disciplines. For example, a recent survey of research articles on spirituality in three medical databases between the years 1962 and 1999 produced 2306 citations (O'Connor et al., 2002). These included quantitative, qualitative, and theoretical (hermeneutical) research methods. Researchers producing the quantitative studies were from epidemiology, nursing, occupational therapy, medicine, and psychology; only a few were from chaplaincy or other theological disciplines. A study of the empirical research in four pastoral journals by Gartner, Larson, and Vachar-Mayberry (1990) showed a small number of quantitative research articles in these journals. Those who are educated in theology have a harder time adapting and using quantitative research methods in the study of spiritual care. One reason may be that pastoral ministry and spiritual care lend themselves to other methods of research.

Qualitative Research Methods

Qualitative research has emerged in many non-theological disciplines as a valid form of research. Some examples are sociology (Adler and Adler, 1994), anthropology, (Miller and Crabtree, 1994), education (Guba and Lincoln, 1994) and family therapy (Sprenkle and Moon, 1996b). Qualitative research methods have also made an impact in pastoral ministry and spiritual care, many D.Min. dissertations utilize a qualitative research methodology. Qualitative research involves a variety of methods. Four are explored here: ethnography, grounded theory, phenomenology, and feminist research. Central to these methods are an open-ended discovery-oriented research question, interviews with a sample, and analysis of the interviews and other forms of the data. While quantitative research seeks to prove or disprove theory, qualitative research seeks to discover theory (Leedy, 1993). The interview method of qualitative research makes it user friendly to many clinicians addressing spiritual care. Case study research is sometimes placed with qualitative research. Other writers place it more in hermeneutical research. Case studies are common in the field of pastoral care and counseling.

Ethnography was developed primarily by sociologists and anthropologists (Newfield et al.,1996). It is considered naturalistic research in that the researchers study persons in their environment and not in a laboratory. The researcher joined the village or cultural group that was being studied. He/she/they became participants in the culture as well as observers (participant-observers). The researcher made copious notes (field notes) on what was observed, interviewed members of the culture to understand the culture from the members' standpoint (dramaturgical interviewing), and gathered other documents and data that revealed the experiences and reflections of the members of the culture (Berg, 1998). All these sources are data and analyzed for meaning (Newfield et al., 1996). Ethnography can be about the total way of life of a culture or a smaller part of it (microethnography) (O'Connor et al., 1999).

▧ A Case Example of Ethnography

In "Making the Most and Making Sense: Ethnography of Spirituality in Palliative Care" (O'Connor et al., 1997a), a team of researchers explored the question: What are patients' and staffs' experience of spirituality in palliative care? The team joined a palliative care team and their patients. They interviewed, observed, made field notes, and gathered materials written by both staff and patients. The data was analyzed and compared according to staff perceptions, patient perceptions, and perceptions from the literature. Similarities and differences were noted and implications offered for clinical work in dealing with spirituality in palliative care. The strengths of this research include the involvement of many researchers from more than one discipline, the involvement of both patients and staff in their natural environments and a comparison with the literature. One weakness is that the staff selected the patients to be observed and interviewed.

Grounded theory has many similarities to ethnography. It is naturalistic research and the researcher enters the environment of the people being studied (Strauss and Corbin, 1994; Raful & Moon, 1996). Grounded theory is defined by Silvia Raful and Sidney Moon as "a methodology based on theory development from data that are collected and analyzed systematically and recursively" (Raful & Moon, 1996, 65). This method relies heavily on data that is recorded and transcribed. This can be taped interviews and/or any written material that can be inductively analyzed for theoretical categories. Emerging theoretical categories from one piece of data are constantly compared with theory from other data in constant comparison. Analysis and data gathering stops when the theoretical categories are saturated. An example is "Pastoral Perspectives in Intensive care: Experiences of Doctors and Nurses with Dying Patients" by Anne Simmonds (1997).

Ethnography and grounded theory are similar in many respects. Both collect data in the field and not in a laboratory setting. Both utilize the notion of the researcher as participant-observer. Both analyze the data using the constant comparison method and both seek to develop theory. The differences are in emphasis. In ethnography, the researcher is participant-observer and becomes part of the group, makes field notes as well as conducting interviews. In grounded theory, the researcher is a participant-observer but is not necessarily part of the group. Field notes by the researcher are not emphasized. Grounded theory emphasizes developing theory inductively from the data. Data analysis and theory construction are central. Ethnography emphasizes that the data articulate what the group believes and does. Developing theory that is far from the participant's views is not a goal of ethnography.

Phenomenology, a form of qualitative research described as social constructionist (Holstein and Gubrium, 1994; Boss et al., 1996), is based on a number of assumptions. Knowledge is socially constructed and not objective. Therefore knowledge is incomplete and tentative. There is a relationship between what is being studied and the researcher. Researchers are not separate from what is being studied. Therefore researcher bias is present in all research. A phenomenon often has various meanings to the various people involved. Different interpretations of a phenomenon are to be expected. Experience is shaped by the language and meaning available to the participants. The researcher is not viewed as the expert on a phenomenon, rather those involved in the phenomenon are considered experts on it.

While phenomenology has many similarities to ethnography in that both seek to understand the phenomenon from the insider's standpoint, phenomenology gives greater emphasis to the meaning and varieties of meaning put on the experience. Researchers utilizing this form of research often articulate their own views and meanings on the phenomenon. One difference between ethnography and phenomenology is that phenomenology does not have to enter the natural setting of the culture being studied. An example of phenomenological research is "Miriam Dancing and with Leprosy: Women's Experience of Supervision in CAPE" (Meakes & O'Connor, 1993).

Feminist qualitative research has developed quite extensively in the last twenty-five years (Olesen, 1994; Avis & Turner, 1995). It is an outgrowth of critical theory research that examines the values and assumptions of the phenomenon being studied (Rediger, 1966). Critical theory uncovers and critiques the theory and values embedded in the culture in which the particular phenomenon arises. Feminist research explores issues of gender with the assumption that patriarchy dominates (Olesen, 1994; Avis and Turner, 1995) and that men have a privileged position in society. There is not equality between females and males on the whole. Men start at a different place and have more access to positions of power and resources. Women's voices are allotted less power than men's (Chittister, 1998). Feminist research values "multiplicity, inclusivity and plurality of voices and methods" (Avis & Turner, 1995, 152). This research is also transdisciplinary and assumes that there are differences between women and men. Feminist research, like critical theory research, is interested in transforming what is being studied. There is an active component to this research. An example of feminist research is Elizabeth Meakes and colleagues, "The Great Leveler: Gender and the Institutionalized Disabled on Faith and Disability" (2002).

Much of the qualitative research on spiritual care in health care (different from pastoral care and counseling) is produced by those outside theology (O'Connor et al., 2002a). Nursing has published most of the qualitative research on spirituality and health. A recent review of qualitative research in four journals of pastoral counseling and care (1993–1997) showed the quantity is small and the rigor is mixed. (O'Connor et al., 2001b) While qualitative research fits well with the praxis of spiritual care, chaplains, and pastoral counselors are producing little. This is certainly an area for development for those in pastoral ministry.

Hermeneutical Research

The great majority of research in pastoral ministry is hermeneutical. Hermeneutical research uses many forms of interpretation theory to understand, critique and/or synthesize interpretations of written texts. Christian theology in the interpretation of Scripture, provides two millennia of hermeneutical research into the meaning of the sacred texts. More recently, this hermeneutical research has expanded to understanding and critiquing interpretations of the Councils of the Church, of theologians, and of the beliefs and practices of various faith groups. This research usually starts with a question or a thesis and then utilizes the written texts to answer the question or to prove or disprove the thesis. Biblical hermeneutics has developed redaction criticism, form criticism, source criticism, etc. Also the ideas of Paul Ricoeur, Hans Georg Gadamer and others in the field of hermeneutics are used.

Hermeneutical research in spiritual care is not limited to the Bible or any other theological material. The texts also include the extensive writings from medicine, psychiatry, psychology, family therapy, sociology, and many other fields, and may also be quantitative and qualitative research that is utilized to support a thesis. For example, Ingrid Bloos and Thomas O'Connor (2002) bring together the practice of walking the labyrinth and contemporary narrative therapy utilizing hermeneutical research.

The methodology of hermeneutical research is not strict but flexible and varied (Schwandt, 1994; Rediger, 1996). One method is Charles Gerkin's narrative hermeneutical approach (Gerkin, 1984, 1986). Hermeneutical research in spiritual care has also expanded the notion of written texts to include human experience. Anton Boisen introduced the idea of the person as a living human document (Gerkin, 1984). Boisen believed that God's revelation is not just in the written texts of Scripture but is also within the human person. Just as the biblical texts need to be interpreted and put into action, so the divine presence within human persons needs interpretation and response. Gerkin expanded this notion of the living human document to include experience between persons. Utilizing a systemic understanding and the hermeneutics of Paul Ricoeur and Hans-Georg Gadamer, Gerkin maintained that God's presence becomes incarnated in the human situation (1984). Differing from Carroll Wise (1966), Gerkin did not believe that God was only present in the person giving spiritual care. God is also present in the person receiving care and God is present in the in-between. This presence produces interpretation by both caregiver and care-receiver. The human person, human action and relationships are living human documents.

In Gerkin's hermeneutical method, the sources for research are threefold: 1) Scripture and all the various theological texts; 2) the non-theological texts; and 3) the case or human situation the interpreter is addressing (O'Connor, 1998; Koning & O'Connor, 2000). Case studies are part of this hermeneutical research method. Gerkin is no reductionist; one of his strengths is that he does not reduce the case or human situation to the interpretations from theology or non-theology. He maintains that the case opens gaps in the interpretations from the written texts. There is always more to the case than the interpretations from the written text can understand and explain just as there is always more to God's revelation in Scripture than we can understand and explain.

While hermeneutical research is a strong tradition in theology, other non-theological disciplines challenge its validity. Paul Leedy (1993) maintains that quantitative and qualitative research are the only approaches that are true research. Most standard texts on research in the social sciences do not even mention hermeneutical research or any of its derivatives. However, some approaches in the social sciences have opened to this form of research.

Spiritual Care Based on Evidence from Research

Much research is never used in the clinical setting. First, clinicians do not read some research. Such research might be in a little-known journal and/or presented at a small conference. The benefits of such unread research go undiscovered. Second, clinicians do not understand some research; a research report written for other researchers, for example, whose findings and implications for clinical work are obscure. Third, some research is not immediately applicable to the clinical area. Clinicians are pragmatic. They usually wonder when reading research: How can the research help me with a particular client or patient?

One way to lessen the gap between research and the clinical world is an evidence-based approach to spiritual care (O'Connor & Meakes, 1998; O'Connor, 2002). Evidence-based medicine began with McMaster Medical School in the 1970s as a way to help medical students and doctors incorporate the best research into medical practice. The clinician began with a question that arose out of clinical practice. For example, a family seeks counseling because the eight-year-old male child has become a behavioral problem both at home and school. The child already has been diagnosed with Attention Deficit Hyperactivity Disorder (ADHD) and is receiving Ritalin. The boy is being supervised by his family physician for the medication. However, the parents and school want help dealing with his occasional outbursts. The clinical question might be: "What is an effective way for the family and school to address the behavioral problems associated with ADHD with a child on Ritalin?"

In an evidence-based method, the clinician begins a search of various databases to seek the relevant research. Relevant databases for this issue are Psychlit, Religion Index, Medline, and CINAHL. Key words for this search are: ADHD, Ritalin, family therapy, behavioral problems, school-age child, teachers, etc., and combinations of these. Such a search produces a number of citations. In an evidence-based method, the search and discussion of the articles are usually done in a group. This is to allow for more critical discussion. In examining the titles and abstracts, the clinical question must always be kept in mind. If the abstract indicates that there might be answers to the clinical question in the article, then the article is deemed relevant. The critical examination of the relevant research involves a number of questions: Is there a research question? Does the research adequately answer the question? If there is not a research question, is there a thesis or a number of hypotheses? Is the thesis or hypothesis adequately proven by the research? What is the design of the research? Does the design match the question or thesis (hypotheses)? Is researcher bias identified? How is it addressed? If the research is quantitative or qualitative, how was the sample selected? Were there any dropouts in the sample? Was the sample large enough? If statistics are used, are they adequate? Does the conclusion match the findings? In three sentences or less, what are the findings of the research? Is the research relevant to the clinical question?

If the research is deemed reliable and valid, then the clinician needs to consider how the research might be implemented. Once implemented, the clinician also needs to evaluate the outcome: "Did the intervention(s) based on the research provide an effective way for family and school to deal with the behavioral problems associated with an eight-year-old boy with ADHD and on Ritalin?"

Certainly, research evidence cannot answer all clinical questions. Nor can all the evidence from research be utilized in a clinical setting. Some research is not clinically friendly. As a result, some clinicians become involved in doing research. A clinician doing research based on the questions from clinical practice can be very helpful to his/her practices as well as the practice of others.

Another effect of the evidence-based approach means moving beyond adherence to one particular therapeutic model. The evidence from the research stems from various therapeutic approaches. An evidence-based approach creates a more eclectic, integrative helper who is constantly searching and critiquing the research evidence and who will change interventions based on solid research evidence. This approach creates a continual conversation between clinical experience and research evidence. Spiritual care then is focused not on a particular helping orientation but on providing the best help and interventions based on the evidence. In the situations where there is no strong evidence, helpers must follow their own clinical wisdom based on intuition, compassion and experience.

Clinical Challenges to Utilizing
Evidence-Based Research

Research and clinical work function in very different ways. Clinical work is oral experience involving conversation with clients. The spiritual conversation includes listening, responding, making decisions, and acting. Conversation is fluid, and unless recorded, impermanent (Ricoeur, 1975). Conversation also involves tone of voice, body language and the physical surroundings, which can never be adequately captured in a written record or audiotape. These non-verbals are vital parts of the clinical work. A videotape is better for capturing more of the non-verbals and setting. However, one is still limited by the camera lens and where the lens is focused.

Another challenge of oral clinical work centers on memory. If the interview is not recorded, then there can be disagreements over what was said. The fluidity and impermanence of oral conversations produce various memories of what happened and what was said. There is no agreed upon text. Clinicians become accustomed to this fluidity and develop skills for dealing with it.

Research, however, results in a permanent written document. One can return to the written text again and again and seek to understand it, challenge it and/or endorse it. This is not possible in the oral conversation. Some conversations make a big impact, positive or negative, on people. However, the listener can never be totally certain whether he/she heard correctly. In marital therapy, one partner may claim that the other said something very negative to him/her. However, the partner being accused of this negative comment has no memory of saying that or believes that the person misinterpreted the comment. This is just one illustration of the big difference between the fluidity of oral conversation and the permanence of the written text.

Another challenge is the nature of spiritual care. Spiritual care is hard to define. There are many definitions of spirituality. In the 2306 articles on spirituality and health (O'Connor et al., 2002), there is no consensus on the meaning of spirituality. It is also difficult to design a randomized control study around spirituality. How would a researcher set up a control group of non-spiritual people and an experimental group of spiritual people? Spirituality has a quality that is difficult to categorize, define, and measure. Clinicians who address spirituality know that there is a certain uncontrollability and incomprehensibility to it (Rahner, 1989).

Clinicians often prefer case studies to large quantitative and qualitative research studies. In the field of family therapy, many of the early pioneers utilized case studies as the method of research for advancing knowledge (Sprenkle & Moon, 1996a). However, most researchers are critical of case study methodology as not producing reliable findings. Again, there is a gap between the needs of researchers and those practicing in the field.

Conclusion

A variety of researchers using a variety of methods are studying spiritual care and spirituality. There is a rich pluralism of research methods in this field. While this area once was believed to be the domain of theologians and church people, now researchers who are not theologians and are not church people are in this field. They are challenging clinicians to provide evidence for pastoral ministry. The conversation between research and clinical ministry has intensified.

◈ Conclusion

THINGS LOOK DIFFERENT depending upon one's vantage point. In the Introduction, goals and ambitions focused the vision and structured the design for the book. In this Conclusion there is a reverse reality. Looking back I wonder: What has become of the objectives set out for the book? and What unique identity has emerged as its special contribution and what further applications can be drawn from it?

I note that some words have come up with great regularity: diversity, perspective, process, context, spirituality, integration—words that spell the conceptual alphabet of this volume. Then there are the metaphors: connecting with one's place, plotting a story, reflecting a harmony, mapping the therapies, straddling different worlds, preparing a homecoming. Together they draw a largely topographical and narrative landscape. Interspersed in the text are tables and figures juxtapositioning a variety of models, dimensions, and styles in the practice of care.

These key words, metaphors, and figures constitute the links that connect the separate pieces into a book. While each chapter can claim autonomy, together they constitute the threads that weave the design and shape the thrust of this volume. The book's message is not so much found in the cumulative impact of its contents as in the integrative perspectives it offers to the practice of spiritual care. I am aware that no person can do integration for somebody else. Yet though a profoundly personal process, it is not an individualistic enterprise. Integration involves dialogue and thrives on diversity in perspectives and opinions. In teaching I often felt, and still do, that if only I present clearly and passionately enough, students will see what I see. To the contrary, experience shows that true learning brings novelty, following uniquely personal pathways, authenticating the student's reality and learning style. My wish is that this book will serve as a catalyst to such integrative processes.

I believe that the main purpose of the book has been accomplished: to present a comprehensive introduction to the clinical practice of spiritual care spanning a theoretical spectrum compatible with a multidisciplinary array of health care providers and therapists. While maintaining their inextricable connection, I am aware of my emphasis on *thinking* therapy rather than *doing* therapy. An interplay between conceptualization and case study organizes each chapter. More generally the distinction is present with Part 2 majoring in theory and Part 3 in practice.

The other main assumption of the book is that spiritual care becomes present in our *being*. The three—knowing, doing, and being—meet in the clinical triad of theory, practice, and the helping relationship. Even though this threesome cannot be dissected or compartmentalized, the core of spiritual care is established in how the caregiver is present both as a connected self and as a self-defined other. The assumption holds that spiritual care is a deeply personal quality of being present to oneself and others, a presence uncompromised by the pressure of performance and attending anxious concerns.

This book has been in process for the last fifteen years, yet does not feel fully finished. More years and work, likely, would not bring the sense of completion. Yet if there were to be an attempt in rounding the project, I would select Part 4, "The Study of Spiritual Care," and expand the supervision section. Initially I envisioned that this volume on spiritual care could simultaneously serve as a manual in supervision by defining a knowledge base, outlining a curriculum for a clinical education program, and profiling the *Helping Style Inventory* (HSI) as the core supervision tool. I believe that the book in its present format can be profitably used this way. While the HSI focuses specifically on helping styles in clinical care, I can see an additional chapter elaborating on the helping relationship in supervision. To stay with the HSI, I see another challenge in developing an HSI assessment tool. I visualize an instrument that can indicate the student's dominant helping style(s) and suggest learning objectives in exploring new directions in the student's personal and professional use of self. Thus the *Helping Style Inventory* that sparked the beginning of this book may, at least in my mind, also forestall its completion.

◈ References

Adams, J., Piercy, F., & Jarich, J. (1991). "Effects of Solution-Focused Therapy's 'Formula First Session Task' on Compliance and Outcome in Family Therapy." *Journal of Marital and Family Therapy*, 17(3): 277-290.

Adler, P., & Adler, P. (1994). "Observational Techniques," In N. Denzin & Y. Lincoln (Eds.), *Handbook of Qualitative Research*, 377-392. New York: Sage.

Anderson, D., & Worthen, D. (1997). "Exploring a Fourth Dimension: Spirituality as a Resource for the Couple Therapist." *Journal of Marital and Family Therapy*, 23(1): 3-12.

Attig, T. (1996). *How We Grieve—Relearning the World*. New York: Oxford University Press.

Augsburger, D. (1986). *Pastoral Counseling across Cultures*. Louisville: Westminster.

Avis, J.M. & Turner, J. (1996). "Feminists Lenses to Family Therapy Research: Gender, Politics and Science." In D. Sprinke & S. Moon (Eds.), *Research Methods in Family Therapy*, 145-172. New York: Guilford Press.

Bagarozzi, D.A. & Anderson, S.A. (1989). *Personal, Marital, and Family Myths*. New York: Norton.

Beavers, W. & Hampson, R. (1990). *Successful Families: Assessment and Intervention*. New York: Norton.

Beavers, W. & Hampson, R. (1993). "Measuring Family Competence: The Beavers Systems Model." In F. Walsh (Ed.), *Normal Family Processes*, 2nd Ed., 73-104. New York: Guilford.

Becker, E. (1973). *The Denial of Death*. New York: Free Press.

Becvar, D. (1996). *Soul Healing: A Spiritual Orientation in Counseling and Therapy*. New York: Basic Books.

Berg, B. (1997). *Qualitative Research for the Social Sciences*, 3rd Ed., Toronto: Allyn and Bacon.

Bergin, A. (1998). In his unpublished *Oskar Pfister Award Lecture*, American Psychiatric Association, Toronto, June 3, 1998.

Bloos, I., & O'Connor, T. (2002). "The Ancient and Medieval Labyrinth and Narrative Therapy: How Do They Fit?" *Pastoral Psychology*, 50(4): 219-230.

Boisen, A. (1936). *The Exploration of the Inner World; A Study of Mental Disorder and Religious Experience*. New York: Harper & Brothers.

Boisen, A. (1960). *Out of the Depths*. New York: Harper & Brothers.

Borg, M. (1995). *Meeting Jesus Again for the First Time*. San Francisco: Harper.

Boss, P., Dahl, C., & Kaplan, L. (1996). "The Use of Phenomenology for Family Therapy Research: The Search for Meaning." In D. Sprenkle & S. Moon (Eds.), *Research Methods in Family Therapy*, 83-106. New York: Guilford Press.

Boszormenyi-Nagy, I. & Krasner, B. (1986). *Between Give and Take—A Clinical Guide to Contextual Therapy*. New York: Brunner/Mazel.

Bowen, M. (1991). "Family Reaction to Death." In F. Walsh & M. McGoldrick, (Eds.). *Living Beyond Loss—Death in the Family*, 79-92. New York: Norton.

Bowlby, J. (1979). *The Making and Breaking of Affectional Bonds*. London: Tavistock Publications.

Bowlby, J. (1988). *A Secure Base: Parent-Child Attachment and Healthy Human Development*. New York: Basic Books.

Bradshaw, J. (1988). *Bradshaw On: The Family*. Deerfield Beach, FL: Health Communications.

Browning, D. (1976). *The Moral Context of Pastoral Care*. Philadelphia: Westminster.

Bryd, R. (1988). "Positive Therapeutic Effects of Intercessory Prayer in a Coronary Care Population Unit." In L. VandeCreek (Ed.), *Spiritual Needs and Pastoral Services: Readings in Research*, 67-68. Decatur, GA: Journal of Pastoral Care Publications.

Buber, M. (1965). *The Knowledge of Man: A Philosophy of the Interhuman*. New York: Harper.

Burr, W., Klein, S., & Associates. (1994). *Reexamining Family Stress: New Theory and Research*. Thousand Oaks, CA: Sage.

Campbell, A. (1981). *Rediscovering Pastoral Care*. Philadelphia: Westminster.

Capps, D. (1993). *The Depleted Self: Sin in a Narcissistic Age*. Minneapolis: Fortress.

Capps, D. (1995). *Reframing: A New Method in Pastoral Care*. Minneapolis: Fortress.

Capps, D. (1997). *Living Stories: Pastoral Counseling in the Congregational Context*. Minneapolis: Fortress.

Carter, B., & McGoldrick, M. (Eds.) (1999). *The Expanded Family Life Cycle*, 3rd Ed. Boston: Allyn and Bacon.

Chittister, J. (1998). *Heart of Flesh: Feminist Spirituality for Women and Men*. Ottawa: Novalis.

Clebsch, W., & Jaekle, C. (1975). *Pastoral Care in Historical Perspective*. Englewoods, NJ: Prentice-Hall.

Clinebell, H. (1981). *Contemporary Growth Therapies: Resources for Actualizing Human Wholeness*. Nashville: Abingdon.

Clinebell, H. (1984). *Basic Types of Pastoral Care and Counseling*. Nashville: Abingdon.

Clinebell, H. (1995). *Counseling for Spiritually Empowered Wholeness*. Binghampton, NY: Haworth.

Cornett, C. (1998). *The Soul of Psychotherapy—Recapturing the Spiritual Dimension in the Therapeutic Encounter*. New York: Free Press.

Corsini, R. (Ed.) (1989). *Current Psychotherapies*. Itasca, IL: Peacock.

de Shazer, S. (1991). *Putting Difference to Work*. New York: Norton.

Derlega, V., Hendrick, S., Winstead, B., & Berg, J. (1991). *Psychotherapy as a Personal Relationship*. New York: Guilford.

Dittes, J. (1999). *Pastoral Counseling: The Basics*. Louisville: Westminster.

Doherty, W.J. (1999). "Morality and Spirituality in Therapy." In F. Walsh (Ed.), *Spiritual Resources in Family Therapy*, 179-192. New York: Guilford.

Efran, Y., Lukens, M., & Lukens, R. (1990). *Language Structure and Change: Frameworks of Meaning in Psychotherapy*. New York: Norton.

Eliot, T.S. (1964). *Collected Poems 1909–1935*. In Weiland, S. (Ed.), *Genesis*. Amsterdam: de bezige bij.

Elson, M. (1986). *Self Psychology in Clinical Social Work*. New York: Norton.

Emmons, R. (1999). *The Psychology of Ultimate Concerns: Motivation and Spirituality in Personality*. New York: Guilford.

Erikson, E. (1964). *Insight and Responsibility*. New York: Norton.

Erikson, E. (1968). *Identity: Youth and Crisis*. New York: Norton.

Figley, C., & McCubbin, H., (Eds.) (1983). *Stress and the Family, Vol. 1: Coping with Normative Transitions, Vol. 2: Coping with Catastrophe*. New York: Brunner/Mazel.

Fleischman, P.R. (1994). *Spiritual Aspects of Psychiatric Practice*. Cleveland, OH: Bonne Chance Press.

Friedman, E. (1985). *Generation to Generation—Family Process in Church and Synagogue*. New York: Guilford Press.

Gabbard, G. (1990). *Psychodynamic Psychiatry in Clinical Practice*. Washington, DC: American Psychiatric Press.

Gartner, J., Larson, D., & Vachar-Mayberry, C. (1990). "A Systematic Review of the Quantity and Quality of Empirical Research Published in Four Pastoral Counselling Journals." *The Journal of Pastoral Care*, 44(2): 115-123.

Gerkin, C. (1986). *Widening the Horizons*. Philadelphia: Westminister.

Gerkin, C. (1989). *The Living Human Document: Revisioning Pastoral Counseling in a Hermeneutical Mode*. Nashville: Abingdon.

Gilligan, C. (1982). *In a Different Voice: Psychological Theory and Women's Development*. Cambridge, MA: Harvard University.

Greenberg, J.R., & Mitchell, S.A. (1983). *Object Relations in Psychoanalytic Theory*. Cambridge, MA: Harvard University.

Griffith, J.L., & Griffith, M.E. (2002). *Encountering the Sacred in Psychotherapy: How to Talk with People about Their Spiritual Lives*. New York: Guilford Press.

Griffith, M.E. (1999). "Opening Therapy to Conversations with a Personal God," 209-222. In F. Walsh (Ed.), *Spiritual Resources in Family Therapy*. New York: Guilford Press.

Guba, E., & Lincoln, Y., (1994). "Competing Paradigms in Qualitative Research." In N. Denzin & Y. Lincoln (Eds.), *Handbook of Qualitative Research*, 105-117. New York: Sage.

Gurman, A., & Messer, S. (Eds.). (1995). *Essential Psychotherapies: Theory and Practice.* New York: Guilford Press.

Haley, J. (1973). *Uncommon Therapy.* New York: Norton

Haley, J. (1996). *Learning and Teaching Therapy.* New York: Guilford Press.

Harris, W.S., Gowda, M., Kolb, J., Strychacz, C., Vacek, J.L., Jones, P.G., Forker, A., O'Keefe, J.H., & McCallister, B.D. (1999). "A Randomized Control Trial of the Effects of Remote Intercessory Prayer on Outcomes in Patients Admitted to a Coronary Unit." *Archives of Internal Medicine,* 159: 2273-2278.

Hill, R. (1949). *Families Under Stress: Adjustment to the Crisis of War, Separation and Reunion.* New York: Harper.

Hillman, J. (1967). *Insearch: Psychology and Religion.* Dallas, Texas: Spring Publications.

Holloway, E. (1995). *Clinical Supervision: A Systems Approach.* Thousand Oaks, CA: Sage.

Holstein, J., & Gubrium, J. (1994). "Phenomenology, Ethnomethodology and Interpretive Practice." In N. Denzin & Y. Lincoln (Eds.). *Handbook of Qualitative Research,* 262-271. New York: Sage.

Jadad, A. (1998). *Randomised Controlled Trials.* London: BMJ.

James, W. (1960). *The Varieties of Religious Experience: A Study in Human Nature.* New York: The New American Library. Original work published 1902.

Jones, P. (1989). *Theological Worlds: Understanding the Alternative Rhythms of Christian Belief.* Nashville: Abingdon.

Karpman, S. (1968). "Script Drama Analysis." *T.A. Bulletin,* 7:26.

Kerr, M., & Bowen, M. (1988). *Family Evaluation.* New York: Norton.

Koenig, H. (1997). *Is Religion Good for Your Health?* New York: Hawthorne.

Kohut, H. (1971). *The Analysis of the Self.* New York: International Universities Press.

Kohut, H. (1984). *How Does Analysis Cure?* Chicago: University of Chicago Press.

Kolb, D., & McCarthy, B. (1980). *The Learning Style Inventory.* Oak Brook, IL: Excell.

Koning, F., & O'Connor, T. (2000). "Left in Pain: Atonement and Transformation in Palliative Care Using Charles Gerkin's Narrative Hermeneutical Theory," *Pastoral Sciences,* 19(2): 191-200.

Kübler-Ross, E. (1969). *On Death and Dying.* New York: Macmillan.

Larson, D., Swyers, J., and McCullough, M. (1997). *Scientific Research on Spirituality and Health: A Consensus Report.* Rockville, MD: National Institute for Health Care Research.

Lazarus, A. (1971). *Behavior Therapy and Beyond.* New York: McGraw-Hill.

Leedy, P. (1993). *Practical Research: Planning and Design,* 5th Ed., 144. Toronto: Macmillan.

Levin, J. (1996). "How Religion Influences Morbidity and Health: Reflection on Natural History, Saluogenesis and Host Resistance. *Social Sciences and Medicine*, 43: 849-864.

Lindemann, E. (1944). "Symptomatology and Management of Acute Grief." *American Journal of Personality and Social Psychology*, 101: 141-148.

Maclean Batts, H., & Mandsley, D. (1981). "From Learning to Teaching: A Learning Centered Approach to the Development of Teaching Styles." *University Education News*, 1: 2.

Mayeroff, M. (1971). *On Caring*. New York: Harper & Row.

McCullough, M., Pargament, K., & Thoresen, C. (2000). *Forgiveness—Theory, Research, and Practice*. New York: Guilford Press.

McGoldrick, M., & Gerson, R. (1985). *Genograms in Family Assessment*. New York: Norton.

Meakes, E., & O'Connor, T. (1993). "Miriam Dancing and with Leprosy: Women's Experiences of Supervision in CAPE." *Pastoral Sciences*, 12: 25-39.

Meakes, E., O'Connor, T., & Carr, S. (2002). "The Great Leveller: Gender and Disability," *The Journal of Religion, Disability and Health*, 5: 37-44.

Miller, W., & C'de Baca, J. (2001). *Quantum Change: When Epiphanies and Sudden Insights Transform Ordinary Lives*. New York: Guilford Press.

Miller, W., & Crabtree, B. (1994). "Clinical Research." In N. Denzin & Y. Lincoln (Eds.), *Handbook of Qualitative Research*, 340-352. New York: Sage.

Minuchin, S. (1974). *Families & Family Therapy*. Cambridge: Harvard University Press.

Minuchin, S. (1997). "The Leap to Complexity: Supervision in Family Therapy." In J. Zeig (Ed.), *The Evolution of Psychotherapy—The Third Conference*, 271-282. New York: Brunner/Mazel.

Mitchell, S. (1988). *Relational Concepts in Psychoanalysis: An Integration*. Cambridge, MA: Harvard University.

Mogenson, G. (1989). *God Is a Trauma*. Dallas, Texas: Spring Publications.

Moore, T.(1994). *Care of the Soul*. New York: Harper Perennial.

Newfield, N., Sells, S., Smith, T., Newfield, S., & Newfield, F. (1996). "Ethnographic Research Methods: Creating a Clinical Science of the Humanities." In D. Sprenkle & S. Moon (Eds.), *Research Methods in Family Therapy*, 25-63. New York: Guilford Press.

Nichols, M., & Schwartz, R. (1995). *Family Therapy: Concepts and Methods*. Boston: Allyn and Bacon.

Nichols, W. (1988). *Marital Therapy: An Integrative Approach*. New York: Guilford Press.

Niemeyer, R. (1996) "Process Interventions for the Constructivist Psychotherapist." In H. Rosen & K. Kuehlwein, (Eds.), *Constructing Realities: Meaning-Making Perspectives for Psychotherapists*, 371-412. San Francisco: Jossey-Bass.

Niemeyer, R. (1997). "Meaning Reconstruction and the Experience of Chronic Loss." In K. Doka (Ed.), *Living with Grief*, 159-176. Washington, DC: Hospice Foundation of America.

O'Connor, T. (1998). *Clinical Pastoral Supervision and the Theology of Charles Gerkin.* Waterloo, ON: Wilfrid Laurier University Press.

O'Connor, T. (1994). "Take What You Can and Dance: Adult Education Theory and the Practice of Pastoral Supervision," *Journal of Supervision and Training in Ministry*, 15: 50-62.

O'Connor, T. (1999) "Pastoral Counselling and Congregation: A Narrative Hermeneutical Approach." *Consensus*, 25(1): 17-28.

O'Connor, T. (2002). "Is Evidence Based Spiritual Care an Oxymoron?" *Journal of Religion and Health*, 41(3): 253-261.

O'Connor, T., Healy-Ogden, M., Meakes, E., Empey, G., O'Neill, K., Edey, L. & Klimek, S. (2001a). "The Hamilton SPE Evaluation Tool (HSET): Is it Any Good?" *The Journal of Pastoral Care*, 55(1): 17-34.

O'Connor, T., Koning F., McLarnon-Sinclair K., Loy V., Davis K., & Meakes, E. (2001b). "Quantity and Rigor of Qualitative Research in Four Pastoral Counseling Journals." (1993–1997). *The Journal of Pastoral Care and Counseling*, 55(3): 271-280.

O'Connor, T., McCarroll-Butler, P., Meakes, E., Gadowsky, S., & O'Neill, K. (1997a). "Making the Most and Making Sense: Ethnographic Research on Spirituality in Palliative Care." *The Journal of Pastoral Care*, 51(1): 25-36.

O'Connor, T., McCarroll-Butler, P., Meakes, E., Jadad, A., & Davis, A. (2002a) "Review of Quantity and Types of Spirituality Research in Three Health Care Databases: What are the Implications for Health Care Ministry?" *The Journal of Pastoral Care and Counseling*, 56(3): 227-232.

O'Connor, T., & Meakes, E. (1998). "Hope in the Midst of Challenge: Evidence-Based Pastoral Care." *The Journal of Pastoral Care*, 52(4): 359-368.

O'Connor, T., & Meakes, E. (2001). Forgiveness and Resentment among People with Disabilities. In A. Meier & P. VanKatwyk (Eds.), *The Challenge of Forgiveness*, 297-308. Ottawa: Novalis.

O'Connor, T., Meakes, E., Pickering, R., & Schuman, M. (1997b). "On the Right Track: Clients' Experience of Narrative Therapy." *Contemporary Family Therapy*, 19(4): 479-495.

O'Connor, T., et al. (1995). "Diversity in the Pastoral Relationship: An Evaluation of the Helping Styles Inventory." *The Journal of Pastoral Care*, 49(4): 365-374.

Olesen, V. (1994). "Feminism and Models of Qualitative Research." In N. Denzin & Y. Lincoln (Eds.), *Handbook of Qualitative Research*, 158-174. Thousand Oaks, CA: Sage.

Olson, D. (1993). "Circumplex Model of Marital and Family Systems: Assessing Family Functioning." In F. Walsh (Ed.), *Normal Family Processes*, 104-137. New York: Guilford Press.

Pargament, K. (1997). *The Psychology of Religion and Coping*. New York: Guilford Press.

Parsons, T., & Bates, R.F. (1955). *Family, Socialization and Interaction Process*. Glencoe, IL: Free Press.

Patton, J. (1993). *Pastoral Care in Contex—An Introduction to Pastoral Care*. Louisville: Westminster/John Knox.

Perls, F., Hefferline, R., & Goodman, P. (1951). *Gestalt Therapy: Excitement and Growth in the Human Personality*. New York: Dell.

Peterson, M. (1992). *At Personal Risk: Boundary Violations in Professional-Client Relationships*. New York: Norton.

Plante, T., & Sherman, A. (2001). *Faith and Health: Psychological Perspectives*. New York: Guilford Press.

Poling, J. (1991). *The Abuse of Power: A Theological Problem*. Nashville: Abingdon Press.

Powell, R. (1975). *Fifty Years of Learning—Through Supervised Encounter with Living Human Documents*. New York: The American Association for Clinical Pastoral Education.

Prager, K. (1995). *The Psychology of Intimacy*. New York: Guilford Press.

Raful, S., & Moon, S. (1996). "Grounder Theory Methodology in Family Therapy Research." In D. Sprenkle & S. Moon (Eds.), *Research Methods in Family Therapy*, 64-82. New York: Guilford Press.

Rahner, K. (1989). *Foundations of Christian Faith*. New York: Crossroad.

Rando, T.A. (Ed.). (1986). *Parental Loss of a Child*. Champaign, IL: Research Press.

Rediger, S. (1996). "Critical Theory Research: The Emancipatory Interest in Family Therapy." In D. Sprenkle & S. Moon (Eds.), *Research Methods in Family Therapy*, 127-144. New York: Guilford Press.

Reiss, D. (1981). *The Family's Construction of Reality*. Cambridge: Harvard University Press.

Richards, P. & Bergin, A. (1997). *A Spiritual Strategy for Counseling and Psychotherapy*. Washington, DC: American Psychological Association.

Ricoeur, P. (1975). *The Rule of Metaphor: Multi-Disciplinary Studies of the Creation of the Meaning of Language*. Toronto: University of Toronto Press.

Roberto, L. (1992). *Transgenerational Family Therapies*. New York: Guilford Press.

Roberts, J. (1999). "Heart and Soul: Spirituality, Religion, and Rituals in Family Therapy Training." In F. Walsh (Ed.), *Spiritual Resources in Family Therapy*, 256-271.

Rogers, C. (1959) "A Theory of Therapy, Personality and Interpersonal Relationships as Developed in the Client-Centered Framework." In S. Koch (Ed.), *Psychology: A Study of Science*, Vol. 3: *Formulations of the Person and the Social Context*, 184-256. New York: McGraw-Hill.

Rogers, C. (1961). *On Becoming a Person*. Boston: Houghton Mifflin.

Rogers, C. (1986a). "A Client-Centered/Person-Centered Approach to Therapy." In I. Kutash & A. Wolf (Eds.), *Psychotherapist's Casebook*, 197-208. San Francisco: Jossey-Bass.

Rogers, C. (1986b). "Rogers, Kohut and Erickson: A personal perspective on some similarities and differences." *Person-Centered Review* 1 (2): 129.

Rosen, H., & Kuehlwein, K. (Eds.) (1996). *Constructing Realities: Meaning-Making Perspectives for Psychotherapists*. San Francisco: Jossey-Bass.

Russell, W. (1991). *Shirley Valentine and One for the Road*. London: Methuen Drama.

Satir, V. (1972). *Peoplemaking*. Palo Alto, CA: Science and Behavior Books.

Satir, V. (1988). *The New People Making*. Mountain View, CA: Science and Behavior Books.

Schwandt, T. (1994). "Constructivist, Interpretivist Approaches to Human Inquiry." In N. Denzin & Y. Lincoln (Eds.), *Handbook of Qualitative Research*, 118-137. New York: Sage.

Selye, H. (1956). *The Stress of Life—A New Theory of Disease*. New York: McGraw-Hill.

Shapiro, E. (1994). *Grief as a Family Process*. New York: Guilford Press.

Simmonds, A. (1997). "Pastoral Perspectives in Intensive Care: Experiences of Doctors and Nurses with Dying Patients." *Journal of Pastoral Care* 51 (3): 271-281.

Slipp, S. (1984). *Object Relations: A Dynamic Bridge between Individual & Family Treatment*. Northvale, NJ: Jason Aronson.

Sprenkle, D., & Moon, S. (1996a). "Towards Pluralism in Family Therapy Research." In D. Sprenkle & S. Moon (Eds.), *Research Methods in Family Therapy*, 3-24. New York: Guilford Press.

Sprenkle, D., & Moon, S. (Eds.) (1996b). *Research Methods in Family Therapy*. New York, Guilford Press.

Stalfa, F. (1994). "Vocation as Autobiography: Family of Origin Influences on the Caregiving Role in Ministry," *The Journal of Pastoral Care*, 48 (4): 370-380.

Stern, D. (1985). *The Interpersonal World of the Infant*. New York: Basic Books.

Stoltenberg, C., & Delworth, U. (1987). *Supervising Counselors and Therapists: A Developmental Approach*. San Francisco: Jossey-Bass.

Stone, H. (1994). *Brief Pastoral Counseling*. Minneapolis: Fortress.

Stone, H., (Ed.) (1999). "A Symposium on Brief Pastoral Counseling." *The Journal of Pastoral Care*, 53 (1): 31-99.

Stone, H. (2000). *Strategies for Brief Pastoral Counseling*. Minneapolis: Fortress.

Strauss, A., & Corbin, J. (1994). "Grounded Theory Methodology: An Overview." In N. Denzin & Y. Lincoln (Eds.), *Handbook of Qualitative Research*, 273-285. New York: Sage.

Sutherland, A. (1995). "Guest Editorial: Research and Pastoral Care," *The Journal of Pastoral Care*, 49 (1): 2.

Tannen, D. (1990). *You Just Don't Understand: Women and Men in Conversation*. New York: Ballantine.

Thielicke, H. (1962). *Out of the Depths*. Grand Rapids, MI: Eerdmans.

Thorne, B. (1992). *Carl Rogers*. Newbury Park: Sage.

Tillich, P. (1951). *Systematic Theology*, Vol. 1. Chicago: University of Chicago Press.

Tillich, P. (1952). *The Courage to Be*. New Haven: Yale University Press.

Tillich, P. (1957). *Dynamics of Faith*. New York: Harper & Row.

Tillich, P. (1963). *Systematic Theology*, Vol. 3. Chicago: The University of Chicago Press.

Tournier, P. (1968). *A Place for You: Psychology and Religion*. London: SCM.

Truax, C., & Carkhuff, R., (1967). *Toward Effective Counselling and Psychotherapy*. Chicago: Aldine.

VandeCreek, L. (1994). "Creating the Question." In L. VandeCreek, H. Bender, & M. Jordan (Eds.), *Research in Pastoral Care and Counselling*, 55-64. Decatur, GA: Journal of Pastoral Care Publications.

VandeCreek, L. (1995a). "Preface." In L. VandeCreek (Ed.), *Spiritual Needs and Pastoral Services: Readings in Research*, vii-ix. Decatur, GA: Journal of Pastoral Care Publications.

VandeCreek, L. (1999). "Professional Chaplaincy: An Absent Profession?" *The Journal of Pastoral Care*, 53(4): 417-432.

VandeCreek, L. (Ed.) (1995b). *Spiritual Needs and Pastoral Services: Readings in Research*. Decatur, GA: Journal of Pastoral Care Publications.

VandeCreek, L., Bender, H. & Jordan, M. (Eds.) (1994b). *Research in Pastoral Care and Counselling*. Decatur, GA: Journal of Pastoral Care Publications.

VanKatwyk, P. (1988). "The Helping Style Inventory: A Tool in Supervised Pastoral Education." *The Journal of Pastoral Care*, 42(4): 319-327.

VanKatwyk, P. (1993). "A Family Observed: Theological and Family Systems Perspectives on the Grief Experience." *The Journal of Pastoral Care*, 47(2): 141-147.

VanKatwyk, P. (1995). "The Helping Styles Inventory: An Update." *The Journal of Pastoral Care*, 49(4): 375-381.

VanKatwyk, P. (1998). "Parental Loss and Marital Grief: A Pastoral and Narrative Perspective." *The Journal of Pastoral Care*, 52(4): 369-376.

Volz, C. (1990). *Pastoral Life and Practice in the Early Church*. Minneapolis: Augsburg Fortress.

Von Bertalanffy, L. (1968). *General Systems Theory*. New York: George Braziller.

Wachtel, P. (1993). *Therapeutic Communication: Principles and Effective Practice*. New York: Guilford Press.

Walsh, F., & McGoldrick, M. (Eds.). (1991). *Living Beyond Loss—Death in the Family*. New York: Norton.

Walsh, F. (1993). *Normal Family Processes*, 2nd Ed. New York: Guilford Press.

Walsh, F. (Ed.). (1999) *Spiritual Resources in Family Therapy*. New York: Guilford Press.

Watzlawick, P., Weakland, J., & Fisch, R. (1974). *Change: Principles of Problem Formation and Problem Resolution*. New York: Norton.

White, M., & Epston, D. (1985). *Narrative Means to Therapeutic Ends*. New York: Guilford Press.

Williams, A. (1995). *Visual & Active Supervision: Roles, Focus, Technique*. New York: Norton.

Winnicot, D. (1965). *The Maturational Processes and the Facilitating Environment*. New York: International University Press.

Wise, C. (1966). *The Meaning of Pastoral Care*. New York: Harper & Row.

Wolin, Steven, & Wolin, Sybil (1993). *The Resilient Self: How Survivors of Troubled Families Rise above Adversity*. New York: Villard Books.

Wolin, Sybil. (1999). "Three Spiritual Perspectives on Resilience: Buddhism, Christianity, and Judaism." In F. Walsh (Ed.), *Spiritual Resources in Family Therapy*, 179-192.

Worden, W. (1991). *Grief Counseling and Grief Therapy*. 2nd Ed. New York: Springer.

Wulff, D. (1991). *Psychology of Religion: Classic and Contemporary Views*. New York: Wiley.

Yalom, I. (1989). *Love's Executioner*. New York: Basic Books.

Appendixes

The Three Core Care Conditions
Rogerian Categories and Definitions

Congruence
Synonyms: realness, genuineness, transparency

- "To be in the relationship without façade and without any attempt to assume or hide behind a professional role" (Thorne, 1992, 36, 37).

- "Whatever feeling or attitude I am experiencing would be matched by my awareness of that attitude ... then I am a unified or integrated person in that moment, and hence I can *be* whatever I deeply *am*" and "if I can form a helping relationship to myself—if I can be sensitively aware of and acceptant toward my own feelings—then the likelihood is great that I can form a helping relationship toward another" (Rogers, 1991, 51).

- "Does not mean that the therapist offloads on to the client all his or her own feelings or concerns; nor does it imply that the therapist impulsively blurts out any passing attitude or intuitive insight" (Thorne, 1992, 37).

Acceptance
Synonyms: unconditional positive regard, non-possessive warmth, gullible caring, interest, respect, prizing, validating, confirming

- "We are afraid that if we let ourselves freely experience these positive feelings toward another we may be trapped by them. They may lead to demands on us or we may be disappointed in our trust ... So as a reaction we tend to build a 'professional' attitude, an impersonal relationship." Thus the need to learn "that it is safe to care" (Rogers, 1961, 52).

- "Can I meet this other individual as a person who is in the process of *becoming*, or will I be bound by his [sic] past and by my past?" (Rogers, 1961, 55).

Empathy
- "A willingness and an ability to enter the private perceptual world of the client without fear and to become thoroughly conversant with it" (Thorne, 1992, 38).

- Not "the accuracy of the therapist's empathic understanding ... but more important the therapist's *interest* in appreciating the world of the client and offering such understanding with the willingness to be corrected" (Rogers, 1989, 171).

- "You are a confident companion to the person in his/her inner world" (Rogers, 1980, 142).

- "If a person can be understood, he or she belongs" (Rogers, 1986).
- "Can I be strong enough as a person to be separate from the other? Am I secure enough within myself to permit him his [sic] separateness?" (Rogers, 1961, 52, 53).

Source: Peter VanKatwyk

Assessment of Core Dimensions of Family Functioning

Focus	Polarity	Extremes		Principle
Family: • **identity**	1. integrity and accommoda-tion	judgmental exclusiveness	indiscriminate inclusiveness	family / couple definition
• **political dynamic**	2. structure and flexibility	rigidity in roles and rules	chaos in rules and leadership	system change
	3. power and equality	coercive control over others	undifferentiated symmetry	relationship intimacy
• **emotional system**	4. attachment and separateness	clinging and dependency	reactiveness and disengagement	self-differentiation
	5. affiliation and boundaries	triangles and split loyalties	isolation and alienation	generation distinctiveness
• **spiritual presence**	6. responsibilities and rights	no caring for self	no caring for others	covenant trustworthiness
	7. idealizing and mirroring	a family clan	a person cult	vocation confirmation

Source: Peter VanKatwyk

Genogram Format

a) **Symbols to describe basic family membership** and structure (include on genogram significant others who lived with or cared for family members— place them on the right side of the genogram with a notation about who they are.)

Male: ☐	Female: ◯	Birth date ⟶ 43-75 ⟵ Death date
Index Person (IP): ▣ ◎		Death = X
Marriage (give date): (Husband on left, wife on right) ☐ m.60 ◯	Living together relationship or liaison: ☐ 72 ◯	
Marital separation (give date) ☐ s.70 ◯	Divorce: (give date) ☐ d.72 ◯	
Children: (List in birth order, beginning with oldest on left) 60 62 65	Adopted or foster children:	

Fraternal twins: Identical twins: Pregnancy: 3 mos.

Spontaneous abortion: Induced abortion: Stillbirth:

Members of current IP household (circle them):

Where changes in custody have occurred, please note:

b) **Family interaction patterns.** The following symbols are optional. The clinician may prefer to note them on a separate sheet. They are among the least precise information on the genogram, but may be key indicators of relationship patterns the clinician wants to remember.

Very close relationship:

Conflictual relationship:

Distant relationship:

Estrangement or cut off (give dates if possible):

Cut off
62–78

Fused and conflictual:

c) **Medical history.** Since the genogram is meant to be an orienting map of the family, there is room to indicate only the most important factors. Thus, list only major or chronic illnesses and problems. Include dates in parentheses where feasible or applicable. Use DSM-III categories or recognized abbreviations where available (e.g., cancer: CA; stroke: CVA).

d) **Other family information** of special importance may also be noted on the genogram:
   1. Ethnic background and migration date
   2. Religion or religious change
   3. Education
   4. Occupation or unemployment
   5. Military service
   6. Retirement
   7. Trouble with the law
   8. Physical abuse or incest
   9. Obesity
   10. Smoking
   11. Date when family members left home: LH '74
   12. Current location of family members

It is useful to have a space at the bottom of the genogram for notes on other key information: this would include critical events, changes in the family structure since the genogram was made, hypotheses and other notations of major family issues or changes. These notations should always be dated, and should be kept to a minimum, since every extra piece of information on a genogram complicates it and therefore diminishes its readability.

Source: From Genograms in Family Assessment
by Monica McGoldrick and Randy Gerson.
Copyright © by Monica McGoldrick and
Randy Gerson. Used by permission of
W.W. Norton & Company, Inc.

APPENDIX 4

The Stages of the Family Life Cycle

Family Life Cycle Stage	Emotional Process of Transition: Key Principles	Second-Order Changes in Family Status Required to Proceed Developmentally
Leaving home: single young adults	Accepting emotional and financial responsibility for self	a) Differentiation of self in relation to family of origin b) Development of intimate peer relationships c) Establishment of self in respect to work and financial independence
The joining of families through marriage: the new couple	Commitment to new system	a) Formation of marital system b) Realignment of relationships with extended families and friends to include spouse
Families with young children	Accepting new members into the system	a) Adjusting marital system to make space for children b) Joining in child rearing, financial and household tasks c) Realignment of relationships with extended family to include parenting and grand-parenting roles
Families with adolescents	Increasing flexibility of family boundaries to permit children's independence and grandparents' frailties	a) Shifting of parent/child relationships to permit adolescent to move into and out of system b) Re-focus on midlife marital and career issues c) Beginning shift toward caring for older generation
Launching children and moving on	Accepting a multitude of exits from and entries into the family system	a) Renegotiation of marital system as a dyad b) Development of adult-to-adult relationships c) Realignment of relationships to include in-laws and grandchildren d) Dealing with disabilities and death of parents (grandparents)
Families in later life	Accepting the shifting generational roles	a) Maintaining own and/or couple functioning and interests in face of physiological decline: exploration of new familial and social role options b) Support for more central role of middle generation c) Making room in the system for the wisdom and experience of the elderly, supporting the older generation without overfunctioning for them d) Dealing with loss of spouse, siblings, and other peers and preparation for death

Source: From Betty Carter and Monica McGoldrick (Eds.), *The Expanded Family Life Cycle—Individual, Family, and Social Perspectives* (3rd ed.). Allyn & Bacon, 1999, p. 2.

Double ABCX Model of Family Stress

The model presents a framework of viewing family adaptations to multiple stressors over time through the use of family resources and perceptual factors in coping. Potential crisis depends on the interaction of the *stressor* (*a* factor) with existing *resources* (*b* factor) and with *perception* (*c* factor).

Resources (bB) Resources are the psychological, social, interpersonal, and economical characteristics of individual family members in interaction with the family and the community. In a time frame, there are two types of resources: those already present and those cultivated in responding to new demands emerging out the *pile-up* of stressors, old and new.

Perception (cC) Here also two kinds of perception can be distinguished. The first c is the initial definition of the stressor by the family on a continuum from hopeless to challenging. The second form of perception refers to how the family over time redefines the stressor in the context of new experiences and the total situation.

The thrust of the ABCX model is a systematic interaction of multiple factors over time directed towards adaptation—a new balance of the family system.

The Double ABCX Model

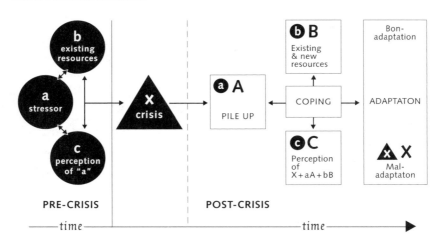

Source: McCubbin and Patterson from Hamilton,
McCubbin, & Figley (1983, 27)

APPENDIX 6

The Flow of Stress through the Family

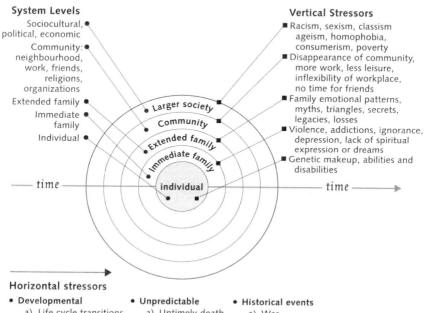

System Levels

Sociocultural, political, economic

Community: neighbourhood, work, friends, religions, organizations

Extended family

Immediate family

Individual

— time —

Vertical Stressors

Racism, sexism, classism ageism, homophobia, consumerism, poverty

Disappearance of community, more work, less leisure, inflexibility of workplace, no time for friends

Family emotional patterns, myths, triangles, secrets, legacies, losses

Violence, addictions, ignorance, depression, lack of spiritual expression or dreams

Genetic makeup, abilities and disabilities

time →

Larger society
Community
Extended family
Immediate family
individual

Horizontal stressors

- **Developmental**
  a) Life cycle transitions
  b) Migration

- **Unpredictable**
  a) Untimely death
  b) Chronic illness
  c) Accident
  d) Unemployment

- **Historical events**
  a) War
  b) Economic depression
  c) Political climate
  d) Natural disasters

Source: From Betty Carter and Monica McGoldrick (Eds.), *The Expanded Family Life Cycle—Individual, Family, and Social Perspectives* (3rd ed.). Allyn & Bacon, 1999, p. 6.

APPENDIX 7

Verbatim Report of Pastoral Conversation

Date: Include three-inch
Pastoral Caregiver: margin for notes

1. **Known Facts**
   Summarize the factual information you had about the
   person(s) before the actual visit. Describe the presented
   or potential "problem" and other relevant circumstances
   that impact the conversation.

2. **Pastoral Pre-Constructions**
   In view of what you know about the situation, what antic-
   ipatory images or pastoral care scenarios came to your
   mind? How do you prepare yourself in the light of what
   you hope will, or will not, happen in the visit? What specific wishes and/or fears are you aware of?

3. **Initial Observations**
   Note the appearance of the person or group of persons
   in the immediate physical/social context of room an circumstances. Describe the beginnings of the pastoral
   encounter and your awareness of yourself and the
   other(s).

4. **Conversation Content and Process**
   Prepare a verbatim account of the conversation to be
   printed on the left side of the paper (not more than two
   double spaced pages), numbering the interactions (P1,
   NA, P2, N2, etc.), utilizing the right margin for noting
   the process and/or personal reactions. Avoid third person descriptions and/or summaries.

5. **Evaluation**
   - The *Helping Relationship*: note the core helping condi-
     tions and the helping style images.
   - The *Presenting Story*: note content and patterns, organ-
     izing themes and metaphors.
   - *Theological Reflection*: what is profound about the expe-
     rience, and what essential meanings and faith issues
     emerge for you?
   - *Learnings*: what stands out for you?
   - *Opportunities* for further ministry?

Source: Peter VanKatwyk

The Helping Style Inventory Map

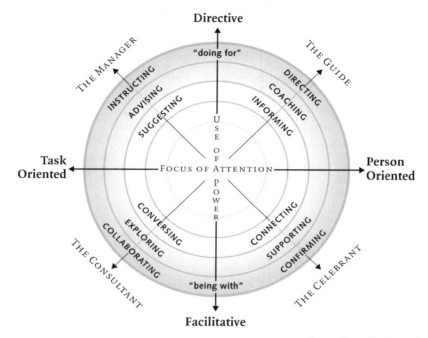

Source: Peter VanKatwyk

APPENDIX 9

Canadian Association for Pastoral Practice and Education/Association Canadienne pour la Pratique et l'Education Pastorales

Code of Ethics and Professional Conduct

▪ Prologue

Members of the Canadian Association for Pastoral Practice and Education/Association Canadienne pour la Pratique et l'Education Pastorales (hereafter referred to as CAPPE/ACPEP) affirm the dignity and worth of each person and respect the right of each faith group to hold its values and traditions. In all ministries, whatever their setting, we hold ourselves accountable to the standards of professional competence and conduct stated in this Code of Ethics and Profession Conduct (hereafter referred to as the Code). As members we knowingly and willingly enter into a membership covenant, the values and beliefs of which are contained within this document. Adherence to this covenant is deemed to be a necessary and vital component of membership (all categories) in CAPPE/ACPEP.

This Code is founded on the following values and beliefs; that

a) We maintain responsible association with the faith group in which we have ecclesiastical standing.

b) We show sensitive regard, given the bounds of our religious affiliation, for the differences of race, culture, nationality, sexual orientation, gender, age and religion of other individuals and societies. We show sensitive regard for the physically and mentally challenged.

c) We are committed to continuing education to enrich our professional competence.

d) We seek out and engage in collegial relationships, recognizing that isolation can lead to a loss of perspective and judgement.

e) We commit ourselves, to be subject to peer review and to abide by such recommendations as may result from such a review.

f) We are committed to the spiritual development both of ourselves, and of those to whom we minister.

g) We strive to manage our personal lives in a healthful fashion and seek appropriate assistance for our own personal problems and conflicts.

h) We provide ministry only for those persons who present problems, issues or educational needs with which we are competent to deal.

i) We establish and maintain appropriate professional relationship boundaries.

Subsection 2
Principles

In all professional matters members of CAPPE / ACPEP maintain practices that protect the public and advance the profession.

a) Practice of Ministry

1. We use our knowledge and professional associations for the benefit of the people we serve and not to secure personal advantage.
2. We represent our category of membership clearly and limit our practice of ministry to the level of our certification.
3. Where applicable, fees and financial arrangements, and all other contractual matters, are discussed at the beginning without hesitation or equivocation and are established in a straightforward, professional manner.
4. We attend to financial matters with due regard for recognized business and accounting procedures.
5. When professional liability insurance is not available through employment, a member maintains such professional liability coverage for the protection of those to whom we minister.

b) Educational and Working Relationships

We, who are in a position of authority and responsibility maintain a concern for the integrity and welfare of our students, supervisees and employees. We recognize the power imbalance that exists and do not abuse the trust of former and current students, supervisees or employees. To this end:

1. We make available to all students, supervisees and employees a copy of this Code at the time of contracting with them.
2. We do not function as therapist/counselor with students, supervisees or employees beyond what is consistent with our role.
3. We do not engage in any form of sexual impropriety in educational and/or working relationships regardless of invitation or consent. Sexual impropriety is defined as, but not limited to, all forms of overt and covert seductive speech, gestures and behaviours, as well as explicitly sexual contact.
4. We regard all forms of harassment between supervisors, supervisees, students or employees as unethical. Harassment is a form of violation which includes behaviour such as inappropriate demands, threats, gestures, innuendos, remarks, jokes, slurs, displays of offensive material, physical assault or taunting about a person's body, clothing, habits, customs or mannerisms. Harassment can also include inappropriate or unwelcome attention to, or comments on, a person's physical characteristics or appearance.
5. We advise our students, supervisees or employees that they may not present themselves as qualified to engage in professional services beyond their level of training, competence and experience.

6. We comply with all the policies and procedures relevant to hiring, selection, evaluation, termination or dismissal that prevail in the place of study or employment.

c) Counselling Relationships

It is the responsibility of members of CAPPE/ACPEP to maintain relationships with clients on a professional basis.

1. Counselling relationships imply a commitment to the healing process. If we are unable or unwilling, for appropriate reasons, to provide professional help or continue a professional relationship, we make a reasonable effort to arrange for continuation of counselling with another professional.
2. We do not solicit clients already in the care of another professional. If a client requests counselling, while in the care of another counselor, it is our obligation to obtain the client's consent to consult with the other professional.
3. We make only realistic statements regarding the counselling process and its outcome.
4. We show sensitive regard for the cultural and religious values of those we serve and refrain from imposing our own values on them.
5. Counselling relationships are continued only so long as it is reasonably clear that the clients are benefiting from the relationship.
6. We acknowledge the complexity of pastoral relationships, and do not abuse the trust and dependency of our clients. We avoid those dual relationships with clients (e.g. business or close personal relationships), which could impair our professional judgement, compromise the integrity of the counselling process and/or use the relationship for our own gain.
7. We do not engage in harassment, abusive words or actions, or coercion of clients or former clients.
8. We recognize that the counselor/client relationship involves a power imbalance. Any form of sexual impropriety or harassment as defined in principles B 3 & 4 with clients (patients, parishioners) is unethical, even when a client invites or consents to it.
9. We also recognize that the residual effects of the power imbalance of the client/counselor relationship are operative following the termination of the counselling. Because of this, any exploitation of former clients in unethical.

d) Inter-Professional Relationships

We recognize that we are part of a network of professional caregivers and are expected to develop and maintain professional relationships. To this end:

1. We seek to support and respect other professionals.
2. We exercise care and professional protocol when receiving or initiating referrals.

e) Confidentiality

As members of CAPPE/ACPEP we respect the integrity and protect the welfare of all persons to whom we are ministering and have an obligation to safeguard information about them that has been obtained in the course of our ministry.

1. All records are stored or disposed of in a manner that assures security and confidentiality.
2. We regard all communications from those to whom we minister with the highest professional confidence.
3. We do not disclose ministerial confidences to anyone, except: as mandated by institutional practice or law; to prevent a clear and immediate danger to someone; in the course of a civil, criminal or disciplinary action arising from the ministry where the member is a defendant; for the purposes of supervision or consultation; or by previously obtained written permission. In cases involving more than one person in the ministerial situation, written permission must be obtained from all legally accountable persons who have been present during the interaction before any disclosure can be made.
4. We obtain written consent of those to whom we provide ministry before audio and/or video tape recording or permitting third party observation of cases.
5. We do not use these standards of confidentiality to avoid disclosure when there is evidence of abuse.
6. When we present material from our ministries in person or in written form, the identity of the recipient(s) of care/counselling or supervision is safeguarded.

f) Advertising

Any advertising by or for a member of CAPPE/ACPEP including announcements, public statements and promotional activities, is undertaken with the purpose of helping the public make informed judgement and choices.

1. We do not misrepresent our professional qualifications, affiliations and functions, or falsely imply sponsorship or certification by any organization.
2. We may use the following information to describe ourselves and the services we provide: name; ministerial designation; the highest relevant academic degree(s) earned from an accredited institution; date, type and level of certification; CAPPE/ACPEP membership level, clearly stated; address and telephone number; office hours; a brief review of services offered, e.g., individual, couple and group counselling; workshops; fee information; languages spoken. Additional relevant information may be provided if it is legitimate, reasonable, free of deception and not otherwise prohibited by these principles. We may not use the initials CAPPE/ACPEP after our names in the manner of an academic degree.

3. We neither receive nor pay a commission for referral of a client or student.
4. Announcements and brochures promoting our services describe them accurately, devoid of all claims or evaluation. We may send them to professional persons and organizations but to prospective or former individual clients only in response to inquiries.

g) Research

When conducting research, we follow the guidelines stipulated by the institution within which that research is carried out. At all times we ensure that the patient, parishioner, client, student, or any other subject is not harmed by the research.

Reprinted with permission.

APPENDIX 10

AAMFT Code of Ethics

Effective July 1, 2001

Preamble

The Board of Directors of the American Association for Marriage and Family Therapy (AAMFT) hereby promulgates, pursuant to Article 2, Section 2.013 of the Association's Bylaws, the Revised AAMFT Code of Ethics, effective July 1, 2001.

The AAMFT strives to honor the public trust in marriage and family therapists by setting standards for ethical practice as described in this Code. The ethical standards define professional expectations and are enforced by the AAMFT Ethics Committee. The absence of an explicit reference to a specific behavior or situation in the Code does not mean that the behavior is ethical or unethical. The standards are not exhaustive. Marriage and family therapists who are uncertain about the ethics of a particular course of action are encouraged to seek counsel from consultants, attorneys, supervisors, colleagues, or other appropriate authorities.

Both law and ethics govern the practice of marriage and family therapy. When making decisions regarding professional behavior, marriage and family therapists must consider the AAMFT Code of Ethics and applicable laws and regulations. If the AAMFT Code of Ethics prescribes a standard higher than that required by law, marriage and family therapists must meet the higher standard of the AAMFT Code of Ethics. Marriage and family therapists comply with the mandates of law, but make known their commitment to the AAMFT Code of Ethics and take steps to resolve the conflict in a responsible manner. The AAMFT supports legal mandates for reporting of alleged unethical conduct.

The AAMFT Code of Ethics is binding on Members of AAMFT in all membership categories, AAMFT-Approved Supervisors, and applicants for membership and the Approved Supervisor designation (hereafter, AAMFT Member). AAMFT members have an obligation to be familiar with the AAMFT Code of Ethics and its application to their professional services. Lack of awareness or misunderstanding of an ethical standard is not a defense to a charge of unethical conduct.

The process for filing, investigating, and resolving complaints of unethical conduct is described in the current Procedures for Handling Ethical Matters of the Ethics Committee. Persons accused are considered innocent by the Ethics Committee until proven guilty, except as otherwise provided, and are entitled to due process. If an AAMFT Member resigns in anticipation of, or during the course of, an ethics investigation, the Ethics Committee will complete its investigation. Any publication of action taken by the Association will include the fact that the Member attempted to resign during the investigation.

Contents

Principle I

▇ Responsibility to Clients

Marriage and family therapists advance the welfare of families and individuals. They respect the rights of those persons seeking their assistance, and make reasonable efforts to ensure that their services are used appropriately.

1.1. Marriage and family therapists provide professional assistance to persons without discrimination on the basis of race, age, ethnicity, socioeconomic status, disability, gender, health status, religion, national origin, or sexual orientation.

1.2 Marriage and family therapists obtain appropriate informed consent to therapy or related procedures as early as feasible in the therapeutic relationship, and use language that is reasonably understandable to clients. The content of informed consent may vary depending upon the client and treatment plan; however, informed consent generally necessitates that the client: (a) has the capacity to consent; (b) has been adequately informed of significant information concerning treatment processes and procedures; (c) has been adequately informed of potential risks and benefits of treatments for which generally recognized standards do not yet exist; (d) has freely and without undue influence expressed consent; and (e) has provided consent that is appropriately documented. When persons, due to age or mental status, are legally incapable of giving informed consent, marriage and family therapists obtain informed permission from a legally authorized person, if such substitute consent is legally permissible.

1.3 Marriage and family therapists are aware of their influential positions with respect to clients, and they avoid exploiting the trust and dependency of such persons. Therapists, therefore, make every effort to avoid conditions and multiple relationships with clients that could impair professional judgment or increase the risk of exploitation. Such relationships include, but are not limited to, business or close personal relationships with a client or the client's immediate family. When the risk of impairment or exploitation exists due to conditions or multiple roles, therapists take appropriate precautions.

1.4   Sexual intimacy with clients is prohibited.

1.5   Sexual intimacy with former clients is likely to be harmful and is therefore prohibited for two years following the termination of therapy or last professional contact. In an effort to avoid exploiting the trust and dependency of clients, marriage and family therapists should not engage in sexual intimacy with former clients after the two years following termination or last professional contact. Should therapists engage in sexual intimacy with former clients following two years after termination or last professional contact, the burden shifts to the therapist to demonstrate that there has been no exploitation or injury to the former client or to the client's immediate family.

1.6   Marriage and family therapists comply with applicable laws regarding the reporting of alleged unethical conduct.

1.7   Marriage and family therapists do not use their professional relationships with clients to further their own interests.

1.8   Marriage and family therapists respect the rights of clients to make decisions and help them to understand the consequences of these decisions. Therapists clearly advise the clients that they have the responsibility to make decisions regarding relationships such as cohabitation, marriage, divorce, separation,reconciliation, custody, and visitation.

1.9   Marriage and family therapists continue therapeutic relationships only so long as it is reasonably clear that clients are benefiting from the relationship.

1.10 Marriage and family therapists assist persons in obtaining other therapeutic services if the therapist is unable or unwilling, for appropriate reasons, to provide professional help.

1.11 Marriage and family therapists do not abandon or neglect clients in treatment without making reasonable arrangements for the continuation of such treatment.

1.12 Marriage and family therapists obtain written informed consent from clients before videotaping, audio recording, or permitting third-party observation.

1.13 Marriage and family therapists, upon agreeing to provide services to a person or entity at the request of a third party, clarify, to the extent feasible and at the outset of the service, the nature of the relationship with each party and the limits of confidentiality.

Principle II

Confidentiality

Marriage and family therapists have unique confidentiality concerns because the client in a therapeutic relationship may be more than one person. Therapists respect and guard the confidences of each individual client.

2.1 Marriage and family therapists disclose to clients and other interested parties, as early as feasible in their professional contacts, the nature of confidentiality and possible limitations of the clients' right to confidentiality. Therapists review with clients the circumstances where confidential information may be requested and where disclosure of confidential information may be legally required. Circumstances may necessitate repeated disclosures.

2.2 Marriage and family therapists do not disclose client confidences except by written authorization or waiver, or where mandated or permitted by law. Verbal authorization will not be sufficient except in emergency situations, unless prohibited by law. When providing couple, family or group treatment, the therapist does not disclose information outside the treatment context without a written authorization from each individual competent to execute a waiver. In the context of couple, family or group treatment, the therapist may not reveal any individual's confidences to others in the client unit without the prior written permission of that individual.

2.3 Marriage and family therapists use client and/or clinical materials in teaching, writing, consulting, research, and public presentations only if a written waiver has been obtained in accordance with Subprinciple 2.2, or when appropriate steps have been taken to protect client identity and confidentiality.

2.4 Marriage and family therapists store, safeguard, and dispose of client records in ways that maintain confidentiality and in accord with applicable laws and professional standards.

2.5 Subsequent to the therapist moving from the area, closing the practice, or upon the death of the therapist, a marriage and family therapist arranges for the storage, transfer, or disposal of client records in ways that maintain confidentiality and safeguard the welfare of clients.

2.6 Marriage and family therapists, when consulting with colleagues or referral sources, do not share confidential information that could reasonably lead to the identification of a client, research participant, supervisee, or other person with whom they have a confidential relationship unless they have obtained the prior written consent of the client, research participant, supervisee, or other person with whom they have a confidential relationship. Information may be shared only to the extent necessary to achieve the purposes of the consultation.

Principle III

▨ Professional Competence and Integrity

Marriage and family therapists maintain high standards of professional competence and integrity.

3.1 Marriage and family therapists pursue knowledge of new developments and maintain competence in marriage and family therapy through education, training, or supervised experience.

3.2 Marriage and family therapists maintain adequate knowledge of and adhere to applicable laws, ethics, and professional standards.

3.3 Marriage and family therapists seek appropriate professional assistance for their personal problems or conflicts that may impair work performance or clinical judgment.

3.4 Marriage and family therapists do not provide services that create a conflict of interest that may impair work performance or clinical judgment.

3.5 Marriage and family therapists, as presenters, teachers, supervisors, consultants and researchers, are dedicated to high standards of scholarship, present accurate information, and disclose potential conflicts of interest.

3.6 Marriage and family therapists maintain accurate and adequate clinical and financial records.

3.7 While developing new skills in specialty areas, marriage and family therapists take steps to ensure the competence of their work and to protect clients from possible harm. Marriage and family therapists practice in specialty areas new to them only after appropriate education, training, or supervised experience.

3.8 Marriage and family therapists do not engage in sexual or other forms of harassment of clients, students, trainees, supervisees, employees, colleagues, or research subjects.

3.9 Marriage and family therapists do not engage in the exploitation of clients, students, trainees, supervisees, employees, colleagues, or research subjects.

3.10 Marriage and family therapists do not give to or receive from clients (a) gifts of substantial value or (b) gifts that impair the integrity or efficacy of the therapeutic relationship.

3.11 Marriage and family therapists do not diagnose, treat, or advise on problems outside the recognized boundaries of their competencies.

3.12 Marriage and family therapists make efforts to prevent the distortion or misuse of their clinical and research findings.

3.13 Marriage and family therapists, because of their ability to influence and alter the lives of others, exercise special care when making public their professional recommendations and opinions through testimony or other public statements.

3.14 To avoid a conflict of interests, marriage and family therapists who treat minors or adults involved in custody or visitation actions may not also perform forensic evaluations for custody, residence, or visitation of the minor. The marriage and family therapist who treats the minor may provide the court or mental health professional performing the evaluation with information about the minor from the marriage and family therapist's perspective as a treating marriage and family therapist, so long as the marriage and family therapist does not violate confidentiality.

3.15 Marriage and family therapists are in violation of this Code and subject to termination of membership or other appropriate action if they: (a) are convicted of any felony; (b) are convicted of a misdemeanor related to their qualifications or functions; (c) engage in conduct which could lead to conviction of a felony, or a misdemeanor related to their qualifications or functions; (d) are expelled from or disciplined by other professional organizations; (e) have their licenses or certificates suspended or revoked or are otherwise disciplined by regulatory bodies; (f) continue to practice marriage and family therapy while no longer competent to do so because they are impaired by physical or mental causes or the abuse of alcohol or other substances; or (g) fail to cooperate with the Association at any point from the inception of an ethical complaint through the completion of all proceedings regarding that complaint.

Principle IV

Responsibility to Students and Supervisees

Marriage and family therapists do not exploit the trust and dependency of students and supervisees.

4.1 Marriage and family therapists are aware of their influential positions with respect to students and supervisees, and they avoid exploiting the trust and dependency of such persons. Therapists, therefore, make every effort to avoid conditions and multiple relationships that could impair professional objectivity or increase the risk of exploitation. When the risk of impairment or exploitation exists due to conditions or multiple roles, therapists take appropriate precautions.

4.2 Marriage and family therapists do not provide therapy to current students or supervisees.

4.3 Marriage and family therapists do not engage in sexual intimacy with students or supervisees during the evaluative or training relationship between the therapist and student or supervisee. Should a supervisor engage in sexual activity with a former supervisee, the burden of proof shifts to the supervisor to demonstrate that there has been no exploitation or injury to the supervisee.

4.4   Marriage and family therapists do not permit students or supervisees to perform or to hold themselves out as competent to perform professional services beyond their training, level of experience, and competence.

4.5   Marriage and family therapists take reasonable measures to ensure that services provided by supervisees are professional.

4.6   Marriage and family therapists avoid accepting as supervisees or students those individuals with whom a prior or existing relationship could compromise the therapist's objectivity. When such situations cannot be avoided, therapists take appropriate precautions to maintain objectivity. Examples of such relationships include, but are not limited to, those individuals with whom the therapist has a current or prior sexual, close personal, immediate familial, or therapeutic relationship.

4.7   Marriage and family therapists do not disclose supervisee confidences except by written authorization or waiver, or when mandated or permitted by law. In educational or training settings where there are multiple supervisors, disclosures are permitted only to other professional colleagues, administrators, or employers who share responsibility for training of the supervisee. Verbal authorization will not be sufficient except in emergency situations, unless prohibited by law.

Principle V

Responsibility to Research Participants

Investigators respect the dignity and protect the welfare of research participants, and are aware of applicable laws and regulations and professional standards governing the conduct of research.

5.1   Investigators are responsible for making careful examinations of ethical acceptability in planning studies. To the extent that services to research participants may be compromised by participation in research, investigators seek the ethical advice of qualified professionals not directly involved in the investigation and observe safeguards to protect the rights of research participants.

5.2   Investigators requesting participant involvement in research inform participants of the aspects of the research that might reasonably be expected to influence willingness to participate. Investigators are especially sensitive to the possibility of diminished consent when participants are also receiving clinical services, or have impairments which limit understanding and/or communication, or when participants are children.

5.3   Investigators respect each participant's freedom to decline participation in or to withdraw from a research study at any time. This obligation requires special thought and consideration when investigators or other members of the research team are in positions of authority or influence over participants. Marriage and family therapists, therefore, make every effort to avoid multiple relationships with research participants that could impair professional judgment or increase the risk of exploitation.

5.4   Information obtained about a research participant during the course of an investigation is confidential unless there is a waiver previously obtained in writing. When the possibility exists that others, including family members, may obtain access to such information, this possibility, together with the plan for protecting confidentiality, is explained as part of the procedure for obtaining informed consent.

Principle VI

Responsibility to the Profession

Marriage and family therapists respect the rights and responsibilities of professional colleagues and participate in activities that advance the goals of the profession.

6.1   Marriage and family therapists remain accountable to the standards of the profession when acting as members or employees of organizations. If the mandates of an organization with which a marriage and family therapist is affiliated, through employment, contract or otherwise, conflict with the AAMFT Code of Ethics, marriage and family therapists make known to the organization their commitment to the AAMFT Code of Ethics and attempt to resolve the conflict in a way that allows the fullest adherence to the Code of Ethics.

6.2   Marriage and family therapists assign publication credit to those who have contributed to a publication in proportion to their contributions and in accordance with customary professional publication practices.

6.3   Marriage and family therapists do not accept or require authorship credit for a publication based on research from a student's program, unless the therapist made a substantial contribution beyond being a faculty advisor or research committee member. Coauthorship on a student thesis, dissertation, or project should be determined in accordance with principles of fairness and justice.

6.4   Marriage and family therapists who are the authors of books or other materials that are published or distributed do not plagiarize or fail to cite persons to whom credit for original ideas or work is due.

6.5   Marriage and family therapists who are the authors of books or other materials published or distributed by an organization take reasonable precautions to ensure that the organization promotes and advertises the materials accurately and factually.

6.6   Marriage and family therapists participate in activities that contribute to a better community and society, including devoting a portion of their professional activity to services for which there is little or no financial return.

6.7 Marriage and family therapists are concerned with developing laws and regulations pertaining to marriage and family therapy that serve the public interest, and with altering such laws and regulations that are not in the public interest.

6.8 Marriage and family therapists encourage public participation in the design and delivery of professional services and in the regulation of practitioners.

Principle VII

Financial Arrangements

Marriage and family therapists make financial arrangements with clients, third-party payors, and supervisees that are reasonably understandable and conform to accepted professional practices.

7.1 Marriage and family therapists do not offer or accept kickbacks, rebates, bonuses, or other remuneration for referrals; fee-for-service arrangements are not prohibited.

7.2 Prior to entering into the therapeutic or supervisory relationship, marriage and family therapists clearly disclose and explain to clients and supervisees: (a) all financial arrangements and fees related to professional services, including charges for canceled or missed appointments; (b) the use of collection agencies or legal measures for nonpayment; and (c) the procedure for obtaining payment from the client, to the extent allowed by law, if payment is denied by the third-party payor. Once services have begun, therapists provide reasonable notice of any changes in fees or other charges.

7.3 Marriage and family therapists give reasonable notice to clients with unpaid balances of their intent to seek collection by agency or legal recourse. When such action is taken, therapists will not disclose clinical information.

7.4 Marriage and family therapists represent facts truthfully to clients, third-party payors, and supervisees regarding services rendered.

7.5 Marriage and family therapists ordinarily refrain from accepting goods and services from clients in return for services rendered. Bartering for professional services may be conducted only if: (a) the supervisee or client requests it, (b) the relationship is not exploitative, (c) the professional relationship is not distorted, and (d) a clear written contract is established.

7.6 Marriage and family therapists may not withhold records under their immediate control that are requested and needed for a client's treatment solely because payment has not been received for past services, except as otherwise provided by law.

Principle VIII

Advertising

Marriage and family therapists engage in appropriate informational activities, including those that enable the public, referral sources, or others to choose professional services on an informed basis.

8.1   Marriage and family therapists accurately represent their competencies, education, training, and experience relevant to their practice of marriage and family therapy.

8.2   Marriage and family therapists ensure that advertisements and publications in any media (such as directories, announcements, business cards, newspapers, radio, television, Internet, and facsimiles) convey information that is necessary for the public to make an appropriate selection of professional services. Information could include: (a) office information, such as name, address, telephone number, credit card acceptability, fees, languages spoken, and office hours; (b) qualifying clinical degree (see subprinciple 8.5); (c) other earned degrees (see subprinciple 8.5) and state or provincial licensures and/or certifications; (d) AAMFT clinical member status; and (e) description of practice.

8.3   Marriage and family therapists do not use names that could mislead the public concerning the identity, responsibility, source, and status of those practicing under that name, and do not hold themselves out as being partners or associates of a firm if they are not.

8.4   Marriage and family therapists do not use any professional identification (such as a business card, office sign, letterhead, Internet, or telephone or association directory listing) if it includes a statement or claim that is false, fraudulent, misleading, or deceptive.

8.5   In representing their educational qualifications, marriage and family therapists list and claim as evidence only those earned degrees: (a) from institutions accredited by regional accreditation sources recognized by the United States Department of Education, (b) from institutions recognized by states or provinces that license or certify marriage and family therapists, or (c) from equivalent foreign institutions.

8.6   Marriage and family therapists correct, wherever possible, false, misleading, or inaccurate information and representations made by others concerning the therapist's qualifications, services, or products.

8.7   Marriage and family therapists make certain that the qualifications of their employees or supervisees are represented in a manner that is not false, misleading, or deceptive.

8.8   Marriage and family therapists do not represent themselves as providing specialized services unless they have the appropriate education, training, or supervised experience.

◈ Index